To Shirley & Lloyd

Wishing you many happy
days in the kitchen
Much love
From us all
Mary. (Waite)
Auckland N.Z.

SIMPLY DELICIOUS

First published by Hicks Smith & Sons Ltd.
238 Wakefield Street, Wellington
301 Kent Street, Sydney

© Hicks Smith & Sons Ltd, 1975.

S.B.N. 456 01860 3

Photoset by John van Hulst, Wellington, N.Z.
Printed by Toppan Printing Co.
Hong Kong.

SIMPLY DELICIOUS

ALISON HOLST

 Hicks Smith
+ Sons Ltd.

Acknowledgments

I would like to thank my sister Clare Ferguson for her illustrations, and the following for their help and cooperation for the photography in this book:

John McNulty
N.Z. Potato Board
N.Z. Egg Marketing Authority
J. Wattie Canneries
K. J. Rew & Co Ltd

Contents

Preface

The recipes in this book are great favourites with my family and friends.

I use the word 'friends' in a wide sense — to include the many women with whom I come in contact in the course of my cooking.

With regular television programmes, radio talkbacks, live cooking demonstrations (raising funds for charities) mall and store demonstrations, competition judging, writing for magazines and newspapers — and my books — I have been able to talk to many thousands of women, from one end of New Zealand to the other, about food, our common interest.

I have gained a great deal from these conversations and letters. I know, first hand, what recipes are most useful, what questions need answering, and of course I find out quickly which of my recipes are most popular, as well as hearing about the ones that aren't! I really enjoy this 'back-chat', and feel that I have been very lucky to have made so many good friends in the course of my work.

As a result, when I publish a book, you can be sure that the recipes have been well and truly tested, and are only included if they have been generally popular.

As my children get older and my life gets busier, I am constantly looking for quicker, easier ways of food preparation. In this book I have put considerable emphasis on 'short-cut' recipes. It isn't 'instant cooking', but I feel that it's a great help to know some good recipes to help you turn a packet of this, or a can of that, into really quick but interesting dishes. I hope you like the recipes and that you and your family find the results simply delicious too.

A.M.H.
Wellington
May 1975

How To Use This Book

If you want consistently good results in your cooking, particularly your baking, you will find it important to weigh or measure your ingredients carefully.

In this book quantities have been given in the 'old' measures as well as in metric measures. In other words, whether you have scales reading in ounces and pounds and use an eight ounce measuring cup, or whether you have metric scales and measuring cups you will be able to use these recipes successfully.

Do keep an open mind about the metric system. When you buy food in kilograms, grams and litres you will quickly become familiar with these new terms and probably find that you want to use recipes giving these quantities.

Wherever possible the recipes in this book give quantities in teaspoons, tablespoons and cups. When you use these recipes use your old measuring spoons and eight ounce measuring cup or metric measuring spoons and 250 millilitre measuring cup. Whichever you use the result will taste and look the same, but since the metric cups and spoons are a little larger you will find you have made a slightly larger quantity when you use them. Unless specified, use medium-sized eggs with 'old' measures and large eggs with metric measures.

Some ingredients, however, have to be weighed. Ounces are given first, followed by metric weights in brackets. These are the metric abbreviations used throughout the book:

g	gram	mm	millimetre	l	litre
kg	kilogram	cm	centimetre	°C	degree Celcius

Do not be worried if you find that the conversions are not consistent. It is impractical to give exact conversions, so approximations must be made. These vary with the food.

Instead of buying a pound of meat, fish, vegetables or fruit you will probably buy 500 grams. This is a little more, but few shopkeepers will weigh or price 454 grams or even 450 grams of food.

Where can sizes are given, more accurate conversions are made because those weights are marked on the cans in stores now. Eventually the can size will change, and the number of grams will be 'rounded off'.

Recipes for baked products, using butter, sometimes pose a problem. For example, 4 ounces of butter is more than 100 grams, but less than 125 grams. In some recipes it doesn't matter if the smaller weight is used, but in others it does, and it is better to use the larger quantity. I have decided which conversion is best, considering each product individually.

For best results when following a recipe, use your old measuring cups and read the weight in ounces and pounds; or use metric cups and read the weight in grams. If you want to weigh the ingredients that I have measured in cups use the conversion chart on the next page. Whichever cups and spoons you use, remember to measure carefully. Level off spoons and cups with the back of a knife — all the spoon and cup measures in this book are level. If possible use a clear graduated cup for measuring liquids and a nest of metal measuring cups for measuring dry ingredients.

Quantities of flour are given as sifted flour because an eight ounce cup of sifted flour weighs four ounces (and a 250 millilitre cup of sifted flour weighs 125 grams). One cup of unsifted flour weighs considerably more, but its weight varies with the degree of packing so it cannot be used as a standard measure.

Standard Non-metric Weights and Measures

The capacity of non-metric spoons and cups and the volume of their contents is measured in fluid ounces (fl. oz.).

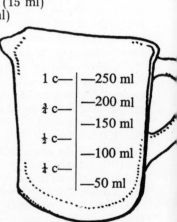

1 teaspoon (⅙ fl. oz.)
3 teaspoons . . . . 1 tablespoon (½ fl. oz.)
16 tablespoons . . . . 1 cup (8 fl. oz.)
5 cups. . . . . 1 imperial quart

The units of weight are ounces and pounds
Equivalent measures and weights

2 tablespoons of sugar or butter. . . . . 1 ounce
2 cups of sugar or butter. . . . . 1 pound
4 tablespoons of sifted flour. . . . . 1 ounce
4 cups of sifted flour . . . . 1 pound

Standard Metric Weights and Measures

The capacity of metric spoons and cups and the volume of their contents is measured in millilitres (ml).

1 teaspoon (5 ml)
2 teaspoons. . . . . 1 dessertspoon (10 ml)
3 teaspoons. . . . . 1 tablespoon (15 ml)
16 tablespoons . . . . 1 cup (250 ml)
4 cups . . . . 1 litre

The unit of weight is the kilogram (1,000 grams)

1 tablespoon of sugar or butter . . . . . . 15 grams
1 cup of sugar or butter . . . . 250 grams
2 cups of sugar or butter . . . . 500 grams
2 tablespoons of sifted flour. . . . . 15 grams
2 cups of sifted flour. . . . . 250 grams
4 cups of sifted flour. . . . . 500 grams

Note
1 teaspoon instant stock. . . . . 1 stock cube

Starters and Fish Dishes

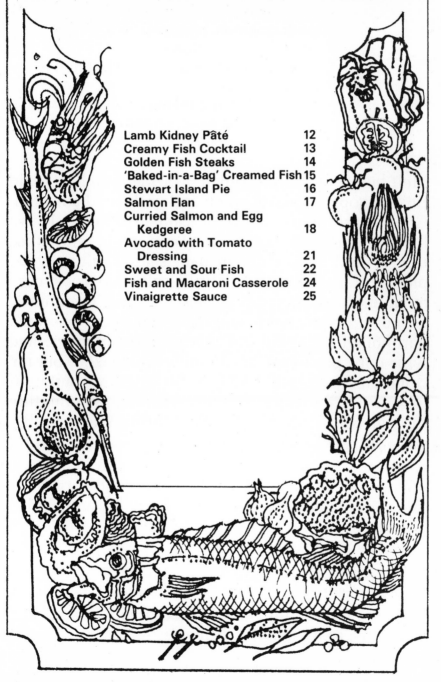

Lamb Kidney Pâté

2 tablespoons butter
2-3 slices bacon, chopped
1 medium onion, chopped
1 clove garlic (optional)
$1/2$ cup chopped mushroom (optional)
4 lambs kidneys
$1/4$ teaspoon dried thyme
1-2 hardboiled eggs, chopped

Melt butter in a large frypan over medium heat. Add finely chopped bacon, onion and garlic and stir well. Chop mushrooms (fresh or canned) finely. Halve kidneys, remove outer skin and core, and slice thinly. Add to mixture in pan, season with thyme, plenty of pepper, and a little salt, and cook over medium heat, stirring frequently, for 5 minutes. Remove from heat and add roughly chopped hardboiled eggs. Put hot mixture into blender, and whir until pieces are small and evenly sized, but not completely smooth. Add a little extra butter if mixture is too thick for blender. Or, put mixture through fine blade of mincer, or through a foodmill.

Season carefully to taste, adding extra salt if necessary. Spoon warm mixture into a straight sided pottery jar in which it can be stored and served, or into a container from which it will be unmoulded before serving. Garnish unmoulded pâté with radishes or tomatoes and parsley.

Pâté should be just firm enough to cut, but soft enough to spread.

Serve it on toast, thin crisp baked bread, or crackers. Try it too, as a sandwich filling.

Creamy Fish Cocktail

1 tablespoon vinegar
2 teaspoons sugar
1 teaspoon salt
$3/4$ teaspoon paprika
$1/4$ teaspoon curry powder
$1/4$ teaspoon nutmeg or mace
$1/2$ cup cream
2 tablespoons tomato sauce
8-12 oz (250-350 g) thawed
   frozen prawns
or 1 lb (500 g) raw fish, marinated

Combine the first seven ingredients, in the order given. Beat with a rotary beater until thick. Do not overbeat — mixture should be thinner than whipped cream. Stir in the tomato sauce.

Make sauce ahead, if desired, but do not mix it with the fish until nearly ready to serve. Spoon fish mixture into glasses, or small individual bowls, or scallop shells lined with lettuce. Sprinkle with paprika.

To make marinated raw fish, select any firm fleshed fresh fish. Cut fish into $1/2$-1 inch (2-3 cm) cubes and cover with lemon juice. Add a few slices of onion for extra flavour. Leave overnight, or for at least 8 hours, in the refrigerator, stirring occasionally. Fish will become white and firmer with time. Drain fish well, remove onion, and combine with dressing.

For texture contrast mix sliced celery, cubed cucumber or green peppers with the fish. The texture of the marinated fish resembles that of lobster.

Golden Fish Steaks

4 groper (or other white fish) steaks
2 tablespoons flour
3-4 tablespoons butter
¼ cup orange juice
¼ cup water
½ teaspoon powdered chicken
   or onion stock
salt and pepper, and sugar

4 servings

Pat fish dry, then coat both sides with flour, reserving the excess flour.

Melt the butter in a pan big enough to hold the four steaks, then cook them over moderate heat, for 3-4 minutes per side, until lightly browned. Lift fish out of pan and add the reserved flour to the remaining butter. Add orange juice, and bring to the boil, then add water and instant stock, and simmer until thickened. Taste and adjust seasoning, with salt, pepper and a little sugar if necessary.

Replace fish steaks in sauce, turn to glaze tops, then cover pan and leave over a very low heat for 10 minutes.

Serve fillets and sauce on boiled rice, with a cucumber or tossed green salad.

For a stronger orange flavour grate. a little orange peel into the sauce, or over the cooked fillets, when serving.

'Baked-in-a-Bag' Creamed Fish

1 packet onion soup mix
1 cup water
¾ cup (1 small can) reduced cream
1-1½ lb (500-750 g) skinless,
  boneless fish fillets
1-2 tablespoons chopped parsley

4-6 servings

Measure the soup mix, water and reduced cream into the roasting bag. Squeeze bag until they are well mixed. Cut fillets into evenly sized cubes or fingers. Drop into bag and coat with sauce. Tie bag loosely. Lie bag on a flattish baking dish, so fish is one layer thick, and bake at 350°F (180°C) for 30 minutes, turning bag after 15-20 minutes. Spoon or tip fish into a serving dish with a border of rice.

Sprinkle with chopped parsley and garnish with lemon wedges.

VARIATION: Replace onion soup with tomato soup or cream of chicken soup.

I produced this recipe after Kirsten came in from a friend's house asking why I couldn't cook fish in a bag, like the frozen product! This recipe is such an easy one it is hard to believe it produces such an excellent result.

If you need something you can assemble really fast, and put to bake while you bathe toddlers and check homework, you can try this. If you work fast, you may even have five minutes to sit down before you serve the meal!

Stewart Island Pie

1 lb (500 g) boned, skinned,
  blue cod fillets*
12 oysters
1 ½ cups fresh breadcrumbs
3-4 tablespoons butter
4 tablespoons flour
1 cup milk
½ cup oyster liquor and dry sherry
pepper, salt and seasoned salt
1 tablespoon butter
½ cup grated cheese

4-5 servings

*Replace blue cod with any white fish fillets
about ¾ inch (2 cm) thick if desired.

Cut fillets into 2 inch (5 cm) cubes, drain oysters, reserving liquor. Sprinkle ½ cup of the breadcrumbs on a lightly buttered shallow casserole, and arrange the fish and oysters over them. Sprinkle with a small amount of grated nutmeg if desired. Melt first measure of butter, add flour, then half the milk. Bring to the boil, stirring constantly, then add remaining milk. After sauce has boiled again add the oyster liquor made up to ½ cup with dry sherry, or a mixture of dry sherry and milk. Boil again, then adjust the seasoning, adding pepper, salt and seasoned salt as desired. Pour sauce evenly over fish. Rinse out saucepan and melt second measure of butter. Toss remaining 1 cup of breadcrumbs in the melted butter, then add the grated cheese. Sprinkle over sauce and sprinkle with paprika if desired.

Bake uncovered, at 375°F (190°C) for 20-30 minutes, until topping is golden brown and sauce is bubbly.

16

Salmon Flan

Short pastry
1 cup flour
½ teaspoon salt
2 oz (50 g) butter
½ cup finely grated
  cheese
3-4 tablespoons water

Filling
3 eggs
1 cup cream or
  unsweetened
  condensed milk
1 can (4 oz or 125 g size)
  salmon
¼ teaspoon salt
pepper
fresh herbs to taste
paprika

4-6 servings

Cut the butter into the sifted flour and salt until the mixture resembles coarse breadcrumbs. Add the grated cheese then the water a few drops at a time, until the dough particles stick together. Chill the dough for 5 minutes or longer, then roll it out to line a 9 inch (23 cm) pie plate. Flute the edges.

Beat the eggs until whites and yolks are combined and add the milk or cream and the fish and its juice. Break up the fish, and add salt and pepper as needed. The amount needed will depend on the fish used. Add herbs such as chopped dill leaves, parsley or chives. Pour the filling into the crust, sprinkle with paprika and bake at 425°F (220°C) for 15 minutes, then at 350°F (180°C) for 15 minutes longer, until the flan is set in the centre.

Serve hot, or reheated, with a salad and warm crunchy bread rolls.

Curried Salmon and Egg Kedgeree

4 tablespoons butter
1-2 teaspoons curry powder
2-3 cups cooked long grain rice
1 can (8 oz or 225 g) salmon, drained
4 hardboiled eggs
1 tablespoon chopped chives
2 medium tomatoes cut in wedges
2 lemons
toast triangles

4-6 servings

Heat a large frying pan (375°F or 190°C on a thermostatically controlled pan). Melt the butter with the curry powder in the hot pan, then add the cooked rice, stirring to coat the grains. Add the drained salmon, broken into chunks. Heat the rice and salmon until the rice starts to turn golden brown on the bottom of the pan and crisps slightly. Spread the chopped hardboiled egg whites, the chives and the tomato wedges over the rice and fish. Keep turning to stop the mixture from sticking. As soon as the egg and tomato has heated through, taste, and season if necessary. Add a little of the liquid drained from the salmon at this stage, if desired. The saltiness of the mixture will depend on the rice and the salmon. Pile the mixture on to a serving dish, sprinkle with the crumbled or sieved egg yolk, and garnish with chopped parsley and lemon wedges.

Arrange buttered toast triangles around the edge of the dish.

Sweet and Sour Fish (p. 22)

Avocado with Tomato Dressing

Tomato Dressing

1-2 tablespoons onion pulp	$^1/_2$ teaspoon salt
$^1/_4$ cup tomato purée	$^1/_2$ teaspoon celery salt
$^1/_4$ cup vinegar	$^1/_2$ teaspoon mustard
2 tablespoons sugar	$^3/_4$ cup corn oil

If you have a blender, simply put half a small, peeled onion into it with all ingredients except the oil, and whir for 10 seconds. Add oil gradually, then transfer dressing to a jar with a lid, in which it can be reshaken if necessary and stored. Blender dressing is thicker than shaken dressing.

To make dressing without a blender, halve an unpeeled onion (through its equator) then scrape the cut surface with a teaspoon to get the pulp. Cut off another slice and scrape again if you do not get enough the first time. Put all ingredients, in order given, into a jar with a screw-on lid, and shake vigorously. This dressing keeps for several weeks in the refrigerator and may be served on vegetable, meat and fish salads.

Check that avocado is ripe — i.e. it feels soft when pressed firmly with finger and thumb. Run knife lengthwise through skin and flesh of avocado, to the centre stone, then twist halves in opposite directions to separate them. Lift out stone by cutting a sharp knife into it near the flesh, then lifting it out.

Avocado halves with tomato dressing

Serve each person half an avocado. Sit each half in a small lettuce cup. Spoon tomato dressing into cavity left by stone.

Avocados with seafood and tomato filling

Proceed as above, but fill cavity with well drained shrimps, oysters, canned salmon, flaked cooked fish, or a mixture of these. Spoon dressing over fish.

Sliced Avocado with tomato dressing

Halve avocados. Peel off skin, then slice. Arrange overlapping slices on lettuce. Pour dressing over.

Sweet and Sour Fish

1-1¼ lb (500-600 g)
  boneless fish fillets

Coating
1 teaspoon water
½ teaspoon salt
½ teaspoon celery salt
½ teaspoon onion salt
1 egg
1 cup dry breadcrumbs

Sauce
2 tablespoons cornflour
½ cup sugar
1 tablespoon soy sauce
2 tablespoons oil
¼ cup vinegar
1 cup water
red food colouring

4-5 servings

Before fish is cooked, prepare sweet-sour sauce. In a medium sized saucepan, mix the cornflour and sugar. Add soy sauce, oil, vinegar and water, and bring to the boil, stirring constantly. Stir in enough food colouring to make sauce bright red. Stand in a warm place, or over very low heat, while fish is cooked.

Cut fish into fingers, or into 1-1½ inch (3-4 cm) cubes. Mix water and salts together in a shallow bowl, then add egg and beat with a fork until white and yolk are blended. (If salts are not mixed with water, they may form lumps when beaten with the egg.) Turn fish pieces in seasoned egg, then shake them, a few at a time, in a paper or plastic bag containing the breadcrumbs. Fry in preheated clean fat or oil (to 375°F or 190°C in an electric frypan) until coating is golden brown.

Do not overcook. The small pieces of fish will be cooked as soon as coating is well coloured. Drain fish and serve immediately on rice. Pour hot sauce over fish and sprinkle with chopped spring onions.

This variation of fried fish is quick, easy and delicious. It makes a small quantity of fish go a long way, and is a good recipe for the mothers of fussy children, since the sauce is poured over individual servings, in quantities to suit all tastes. Buy skinned and boned fillets, or pay less and process them yourself. Remember too, that lesser known fish varieties are cheaper, but good. I have tried this recipe with many different fish and found them all perfectly satisfactory. Experiment for yourself, but remember not to overcook the fish. This will toughen, dry out, and ruin it.

Leave out the red food colouring if it bothers you. In Chinatown in San Francisco we ate many red sweet and sour fish mixtures. It took me some time to find that the colouring often came out of a bottle! It does make the sauce look interesting, so I do it too — even though I feel I am cheating a little. Try it, and see for yourself.

Fish and Macaroni Casserole

1 lb (500 g) raw fish
  fillets
2-3 hardboiled eggs
1/2 cup uncooked
  macaroni
1 tablespoon chopped
  spring onion leaves

6 servings

Sauce
3 tablespoons butter
3 tablespoons flour
1 1/2 cups liquid
1/4 cup finely grated
  cheese
1/2 teaspoon salt
parsley

Use one of the cheaper fish varieties. It is not necessary to select skinless boneless fillets, as skin and bone may be easily removed after cooking.

Place fish on a piece of buttered foil and season well with pepper, salt, a little lemon rind or juice and butter. Wrap tightly in foil sealing the edges, and place in a covered frypan in a little water. Bring to the boil, then simmer for 2 minutes, then turn, return it to the boil and leave it to stand for 5-10 minutes. Increase the times if fillets are thick. Fish is cooked as soon as it is milky white, and the flesh flakes easily. Drain off the liquid and save it — making it up to 1½ cups with milk — lift off and discard any skin, then flake the fish with 2 forks, lifting out any bones. Keep the pieces of fish chunky.

Hardboil the eggs, halve them and separate the whites from the yolks. Cook the macaroni and mix it with the fish and the chopped egg whites. Add the chopped chives. Make the sauce by melting the butter, adding the flour and stirring in the mixture of milk and fish liquor. Add ½ cup liquid at a time, stirring well and boiling before the next addition. Add the salt and cheese, stir well, and remove from the heat immediately.

Place half the fish, egg and macaroni mixture in a casserole dish and cover with half the sauce, then repeat with the remaining ingredients. Cover the dish and heat at 350°F (180°C) until all the ingredients are heated through (20-30 minutes).

Remove the lid, crumble the yolks over the surface of the hot mixture and garnish with parsley. For extra colour, add a little paprika.

Vinaigrette Sauce

$1/4$ **cup chopped raw red pepper**
   (or canned pimento)
$1/4$ **cup capers**
1 clove garlic
2 teaspoons salt
$1/4$ **teaspoon pepper**
$1/2$ **teaspoon dried tarragon**
$1/2$ **teaspoon dill leaves**
2 cups corn oil
$1/2$ **cup malt vinegar**
$1/4$ **cup dry sherry or dry wine**
1-2 tablespoons chopped parsley
1 tablespoon chopped gherkin

Select a jar with a tight fitting lid which will hold about 3 cups of liquid. Finely chop the red pepper or canned pimento. If neither of these are available use raw green pepper. Chop the capers if desired. This is not really necessary, since they tend to mash anyway, when the sauce is shaken. Put peppers and capers in jar. Chop the garlic very finely. Add part of the salt to the garlic while chopping it, if desired. Put in jar with the rest of the salt and the remaining

25

ingredients. Cover and shake well. Refrigerate and shake well before use.

Just before use, add to each ½ cup
   1-2 tablespoons finely chopped parsley
   1 tablespoon finely chopped gherkin
Finely chopped hardboiled egg may also be added just before serving.

NOTE — Replace dried tarragon and dill leaves with the fresh herbs, if these are available. Use 1-2 teaspoons of the chopped fresh leaves.

This dressing can also be served with raw tomatoes, cucumber, lettuce and other salad vegetables, or with canned meat, fish or hardboiled eggs.

It's always a good feeling when one knows there is a carefully selected stack of packets and cans in the store cupboard so that 'instant meals' for unexpected guests can be produced when necessary.

Food purchased like this often needs dressing up for extra flavours, texture and character. Canned meat or salmon and canned asparagus are good standbys for a quick meal. If you find some tasty homemade chutney or pickle in your preserves cupboard, and an interesting dressing already mixed in the refrigerator, the canned food will be much more appealing. Add crisp cold lettuce and tomatoes, and serve a basket of crusty hot rolls (quickly thawed from the freezer) and you've a meal to be proud of!

This sauce or dressing — call it what you will — is not the traditional French recipe, but is a very useful addition to this sort of meal. It is simply delicious over asparagus, but is equally as good with other cold cooked vegetables.

Since it keeps indefinitely, I make it in the quantities given and store it in a covered jar in the refrigerator. I try to plan ahead and cook double quantities of vegetables such as carrots, peas, corn, beans or cauliflower the day before I plan a cold meal. I drain the vegetables, serve the ones for the hot meal, then shake my dressing jar and pour ¼-½ cup of dressing over them. Cover them and leave them to stand in the dressing in the refrigerator, until the next night.

When I need Asparagus Vinaigrette at short notice, I drain the can into a flameproof serving dish, heat it on top of the stove, then pour off the liquid and pour over my sauce. If this is left to stand for 10-15 minutes, it will have cooled to room temperature. (We prefer cooked, cold vegetables at room temperature rather than straight from the refrigerator, because they have more flavour, but in hot weather vegetables left 24 hours or more after cooking should be refrigerated, then left to stand at room temperature for 15-20 minutes so there is not a chance of spoilage.)

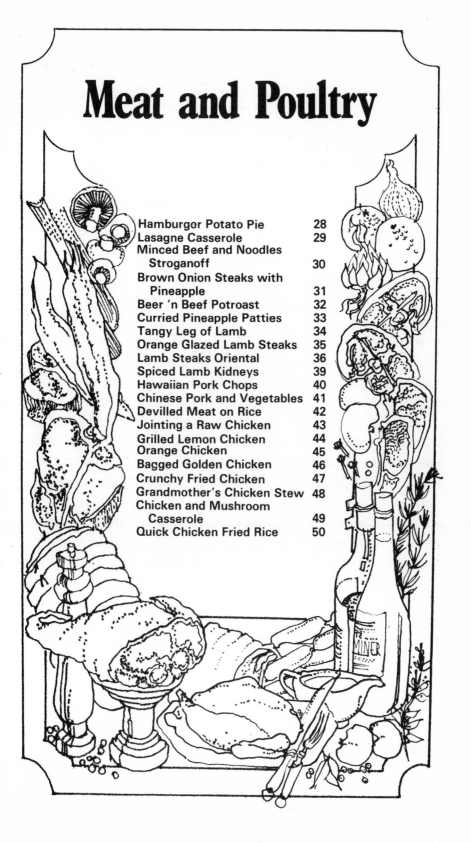

Meat and Poultry

Hamburger Potato Pie

1 lb (500 g) minced beef
1 onion, finely chopped
1 egg
2 tablespoons tomato sauce
1 tablespoon instant beef stock
1 teaspoon worcestershire sauce
1 lb (500 g) potatoes, grated and
  squeezed
1/2 cup cornflakes
1/2-1 cup grated cheese

4-5 servings

Mix together in a large bowl the minced beef and onion. (Grate onion instead of chopping it if preferred.) Add the egg, tomato sauce, instant stock and worcestershire sauce and mix thoroughly. Scrub or thinly peel the potatoes, then grate them, (using the same size holes on the grater that you use for cheese) on to an old tea towel. Squeeze most of the liquid from the potatoes, then mix them with the other ingredients. Press mixture lightly into a greased baking dish, sprinkle with cornflakes, then grated cheese, and bake, uncovered, at 350°F (180°C) for 1-1½ hours.

NOTE — The potatoes will brown if they are grated before they are mixed with the other ingredients. Do not prepare them before you need them.

This useful and economical recipe may be cooked for large numbers in roasting pans. It is firm enough to cut in squares, and tastes good with tomato sauce poured over each piece. This is a good recipe for a child (or husband) to prepare sometime when you plan to keep out of the kitchen! The cornflakes may be replaced by another pre-cooked cereal, or left out altogether. Small quantities of herbs or spices may be added for variety.

Lasagne Casserole

8 oz (225 g) lasagne noodles
1 large onion, chopped
1 lb (500 g) minced beef
¼ teaspoon basil or thyme
1 can (2 cup size) tomato soup
2 cups grated cheese
1 tablespoon butter
1 tablespoon flour
1 cup milk
1 egg

4-5 servings

Boil lasagne in plenty of boiling salted water until just tender. Drain, leaving a few tablespoons of water in pan. Add a tablespoon of butter or oil and shake pan so noodles will not stick together. In a large pan brown the onion and mince, add basil or thyme and tomato soup. Bring to boil, then turn off. In an ovenware dish about 9 inches (23 cm) square, put half the meat sauce. Cover with half the noodles, then sprinkle over half the cheese. Repeat with the remaining meat, noodles, and cheese.

In saucepan in which noodles cooked, melt the butter, add flour and a little salt and pepper. Stir in milk in three parts, boiling between additions. Remove from heat and beat in egg, then pour this evenly over the cheese. Bake uncovered, at 350°F (180°C) for 1 hour. Leave to stand for 5 minutes before cutting in pieces. Serve each piece carefully with a fish slice.

For an easy buffet meal, serve this with green beans and/or green salad, and hot bread rolls.

Minced Beef and Noodles Stroganoff

4-5 oz (125 g) egg noodles
3-4 tablespoons butter
1 large onion, finely chopped
1 clove garlic, thinly sliced
8 oz (250g) mushrooms, thickly sliced*
1 lb (500g) minced beef
1 tablespoon flour
1 cup tomato purée
1/2 cup dry red wine
1 cup water
1 tablespoon instant beef stock
1 teaspoon salt
pepper
1 cup cultured sour cream
1/2 cup grated cheese

*For best results use button mushrooms

4-5 servings

Cook the noodles in plenty of boiling salted water until just tender, then drain.

In a large pan melt the butter, add onion, then garlic, then mushrooms. Allow to brown lightly, stirring frequently. Add beef, and stir until no longer pink. Stir in flour, tomato purée, wine, water and seasoning. Simmer 10 minutes, then remove from heat and stir in sour cream. In a lightly greased casserole spread 1/3 meat sauce. Cover with half the drained noodles. Repeat. Cover second layer of noodles with remaining meat sauce. Sprinkle with grated cheese then bake uncovered for 30 minutes. Serve with bread rolls and a tossed green salad or coleslaw.

Brown Onion Steaks with Pineapple

1-1½ lb (500-750 g) blade steak
1 packet brown onion sauce mix
1 small can (1 cup size) pineapple rings
½ teaspoon worcestershire sauce

4 servings

Select a shallow casserole dish just large enough to hold the meat in one layer. Cut the meat into serving sized pieces, and place in casserole. Sprinkle with the dry sauce mix. Strain juice from pineapple and make up to 1 cup with water. Add worcestershire sauce and pour over steak. If lid does not fit tightly, place a piece of foil under it. Cover and bake at 300°F (150°C) for 30 minutes, then turn steak in sauce and bake for 45 minutes longer, until meat is tender. Place pineapple slices on steaks during last 10 minutes of cooking or fry them gently in 1 teaspoon of butter and 1 teaspoon of sugar until they are lightly browned. Garnish pineapple—topped steaks with parsley.

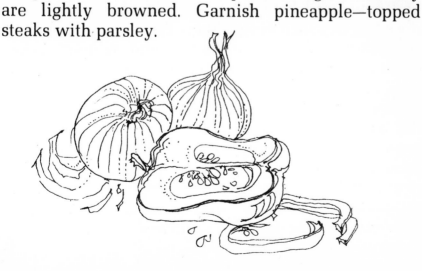

Beer'n Beef Potroast

3-4 lb (1 1/2-2 g) piece chuck
   or bolar steak
1/2 teaspoon ginger
2 tablespoons flour
2-3 tablespoons butter
1 tablespoon oil
2 large onions, sliced
2 teaspoons sugar
1 1/2 cups beer
2 teaspoons instant beef stock
thyme and pepper
cornflour and water paste

Pat piece of steak dry, then mix ginger and flour, and coat meat with this mixture.

Melt butter and oil and brown meat in a heavy frying pan, turning frequently to get an even colour.

Remove from pan to a casserole dish. Add sliced onions and sugar to remaining fat in the pan. Cook gently, stirring frequently, until onions are evenly browned. Transfer to casserole with meat. Add beer and powdered beef stock to frying pan, warm it to dissolve any drippings, then pour this over beef. Sprinkle with a little thyme and pepper, cover tightly and bake at 300°F (150°C) for 1½ hours, or until meat is tender, basting occasionally. Do not overcook. Remove meat from casserole dish, strain off fat and thicken sauce if necessary. Adjust seasoning. Slice meat fairly thinly across the grain.

Curried Pineapple Patties

1 lb (500 g) sausagemeat
2 tablespoons butter
1-2 teaspoons curry powder
1 large onion, chopped
2 teaspoons flour
1 cup crushed pineapple
1-2 tablespoons pineapple juice

4 servings

Form sausagemeat into 8-10 patties with wet hands. Melt butter in a large frying pan and brown patties over moderate heat. Turn patties and add curry powder and chopped onion. Stir in flour, lower heat then add crushed pineapple, cover and cook gently for 5 minutes. Turn patties, add a little extra liquid (water or pineapple juice) if all liquid has evaporated, and leave over very low heat for 5 minutes longer.

Serve on rice, or with mashed potatoes and any green vegetable.

Tangy Leg of Lamb

1 boned leg of lamb
1 small clove garlic
$\frac{1}{2}$ onion, chopped finely
$\frac{1}{2}$ cup chopped mushrooms
$\frac{1}{2}$ lemon, grated rind and juice
1 tablespoon powdered
   chicken stock
2 tablespoons cornflour
2 cups water

Trim any excess fat from leg. Slice garlic thinly and put pieces inside lamb. Roll meat, and tie securely. Place in an uncovered roasting dish (without any extra fat) and cook at 325°F (160°C) for 2½ hours. Add finely chopped onions and mushrooms to the pan and mix well with pan drippings. Cook 30 minutes longer then lift out meat and keep it warm, and drain off fat from pan drippings, onion and mushrooms. Add lemon rind and juice and chicken stock to drippings, mix cornflour with water and add. Bring to boil, stirring constantly, then simmer 5 minutes and adjust seasonings. Remove string then slice meat thickly and serve garnished with parsley and lemon slices cut from the remaining half lemon. Serve with new potatoes, young carrots and green peas or beans.

NOTE — Do not cover pan at any stage of cooking. Gravy should be a rich brown colour, with pieces of onion and mushroom through it.

Orange Glazed Lamb Steaks

4 lamb steaks
1 tablespoon butter
1 tablespoon oil
1 orange, grated rind and juice
2 teaspoons honey
nutmeg
onion or garlic salt
pepper

Trim leg steaks, removing bone if necessary. Snip edges to stop steaks curling during cooking. Heat butter and oil in a large frying pan. Add lamb steaks and cook over high heat for 5 minutes per side, until well browned. Remove meat from pan and keep hot. Add orange juice made up to ½ cup with water and the finely grated orange rind and honey, to butter in pan. Add a little freshly ground nutmeg, onion or garlic salt and pepper to taste. Heat gently until glaze is syrupy, then turn cooked steaks to coat them in it. Serve immediately, with new potatoes, mashed potatoes or noodles, and green beans or broccoli.

VARIATION: For minted orange lamb steaks, sprinkle glazed steaks with finely chopped mint.

Steaks cut from a leg of lamb are lean and meaty. Although they can be cooked in many ways, I like them best when quickly cooked in a greased frying pan, or browned under a hot grill. In these two recipes the basic cooking method is the same, but the marinade, sauce and glaze produce quite different results.

Lamb Steaks Oriental

4 lamb steaks
1/2 teaspoon ground ginger
2 teaspoons brown sugar
1/2 teaspoon garlic salt
2 teaspoons soy sauce
2 teaspoons sherry
2 tablespoons oil
2 onions, sliced
2 stalks celery, sliced
1 red (or green) pepper
1 tablespoon flour
2 teaspoons instant stock
1/2 cup water

Trim any fat from the edges of the steaks. Cut out bones and snip edges. Mix sugar, ginger, garlic salt, soy sauce and sherry in a shallow dish. Turn meat in this mixture. Leave to marinate while preparing vegetables. Heat oil in a medium sized frypan. Halve onions lengthwise then cut crosswise into strips. Cook in oil over moderate heat. Add sliced celery and the pepper seeded and cut like the onion. Coat all vegetables with oil, cover pan and cook slowly for about 10 minutes.

In a second pan heat a thin film of oil, remove lamb from marinade, pat dry, and cook over moderate heat, allowing about 5 minutes for each side. Add flour to vegetables, then mix instant stock and water with remaining marinade. Add to vegetables, stir until boiling, then cover and simmer for 5 minutes.

Serve sauce over steaks.

Spiced Lamb Kidneys

1 lb (500 g) lambs kidneys
2 rashers bacon
2 large onions
2 tablespoons butter
1 tablespoon flour
1 teaspoon dry mustard
1 teaspoon paprika
1 teaspoon sugar
1/2 teaspoon mixed herbs
1/2 teaspoon curry powder
1/2 teaspoon salt
1/2 cup tomato purée
1/2 cup water or wine

4-5 servings

Halve kidneys, cut out cores, then cut each piece in three or four pieces. Stand kidneys in 2 cups water acidified with 1 tablespoon vinegar while sauce is cooked. Chop bacon into small pieces, and lightly brown it in a medium sized saucepan. Add chopped onions and butter and cook for 2-3 minutes, until onions are transparent. Add flour and stir over medium heat until flour browns lightly, then stir in seasonings and herbs. Add tomato and water or wine. Stir until sauce boils, then lower heat and simmer very gently for 15 minutes.

Drain kidneys and add to sauce. Leave over very low heat for 30 minutes then thicken sauce with cornflour paste if necessary.

Serve, sprinkled generously with chopped parsley, on boiled rice.

Crunchy Fried Chicken (p. 47)

Hawaiian Pork Chops

1 ½ lb (750 g) pork chops
½ teaspoon celery salt
shake pepper
1 medium sized onion
¾ cup crushed pineapple
1 teaspoon soy sauce

4 servings

Season chops on both sides with celery salt and pepper. Chop the onions finely. Lie a roasting bag on a flat (sponge roll) tin or baking dish. Spread the chopped onion evenly in the bag. Lie the seasoned chops on the onion, one layer thick. Measure the crushed pineapple and add the soy sauce to it. (Do not drain off pineapple juice.) Spoon pineapple mixture over the chops so the juice runs under them, with the onion, and the crushed pineapple lies on top.

Close the bag loosely with the tie provided, leaving a finger sized hole so steam can escape during cooking.

Bake at 350°F (180°C) for 45 minutes. Slit bag and turn back sides, and raise heat to 375°F (190°C). Bake uncovered for 15 minutes, or until fat at edge of chops is golden brown.

NOTE — Use pork fingers instead of pork chops, if desired. Increase cooking time by 10-15 minutes.

Pork chops and pork fingers cook without drying out in the clear bags that withstand oven temperatures. It is not necessary to fry the chops to brown them before they are bagged, but for best results the bag should be slit and turned back for the last 10-15 minutes of cooking, so the fat under the rind or skin of the pork can brown.

Chinese Pork and Vegetables

8 oz (250 g) pork schnitzel or pork fillet
2 tablespoons cooking oil
1 clove garlic
2 or 3 thin slices ginger root
1-2 cups shredded cabbage
1 cup sliced button mushrooms (optional)
1 green or red pepper, sliced (optional)
4 spring onions
1/4 can bamboo shoots (optional)
1/4 cup water
1 tablespoon cornflour
1 tablespoon sherry
1 tablespoon brown sugar
1 tablespoon instant beef stock
1/2 cup water

2-3 servings

Cut pork into very thin pieces. This is easier to do if meat is chilled in icebox or deep freezer for 10-15 minutes before cutting. Brown meat in oil in a large hot frying pan. Add thinly sliced garlic and ginger when meat is partly cooked. Add shredded cabbage, toss to coat with oil, then add remaining vegetables. Add 1st measure of water, and cover pan so meat and vegetables steam while remaining ingredients are mixed to a paste in a small container. Remove lid, lower heat, and add paste, stirring constantly. Coat meat and vegetables with glaze. If necessary, thin it with a little extra water.

Serve immediately, on noodles or rice.

Any fairly lean piece of raw pork can be sliced very thinly and used for this recipe. Everyday vegetables such as onions, celery and cauliflower may replace the mushrooms, pepper and bamboo shoots. Do not overcook the mixture or the meat will toughen.

Devilled Meat on Rice

2-3 tablespoons butter
2 onions, sliced
2-3 stalks celery, sliced
1 large apple, sliced
1 teaspoon curry powder
¼ cup plum or apricot jam
2 tablespoons vinegar
1 tablespoon instant beef stock
2 teaspoons soy sauce
1½ cups water
1 tablespoon cornflour
2-3 cups cold roast or potroast beef, lamb
    or pork
1-2 tablespoons chopped parsley

4-6 servings

Melt butter in a large frying pan. Cook onion, celery and apple gently in it for 5 minutes. Add curry powder, stir well, then add jam, vinegar, stock powder, soy sauce and nearly all the water. Cover and simmer for 5 minutes. Thicken with remaining water mixed with cornflour. Add finely diced cooked meat, mix well, and leave to stand over a very low heat for 3-5 minutes longer. Do not let mixture boil after meat has been added. Sprinkle with parsley and serve on rice, with green peas and tomatoes.

NOTE —Replace jam with brown sugar if desired. Replace jam and vinegar with relish or chutney.

This is a well flavoured mixture in which any cold meat may be reheated. The meat should be added after the rest of the mixture is cooked, since it will toughen if warmed for too long, or to a high temperature. The sauce has a dark brown colour and looks most attractive when served on rice with bright vegetables.

Jointing a Raw Chicken

(1) Remove the wings
Hold the bird by a wing tip and lift it off the bench. Starting from the breast side, cut through the skin and flesh ½ inch (2 cm) closer to the body than where the wing appears to join it. Cut off the wing tip. Cut the wing in two if the bird is large.

(2) Cut off the legs
Put the chicken on its back. Press the legs outwards and down, cutting through the skin between legs and body. Bend the legs back until the joints crack then cut through the flesh. Divide each leg into thigh and drumstick.

(3) Remove the lower back
Cut through the thin skin to the backbone, below the rib cage. Bend the body back until the backbone breaks. Cut through remaining flesh. Cut through the band of skin under the vent, then with skin side up, push this joint against the board to make it lie flat. Trim off skin flaps and fat.

(4) Separate the breast from the upper back
Look inside the rib cage to see where the ribs bend. Cut along this line from the inside out. Cut through the bigger bones near the neck. Press upper back flat as above.

(5)
Flatten breast then bend it from front to back until breastbone breaks. Cut in two crosswise at this point. Cut each half lengthwise in a big bird. This gives 12 or 14 pieces. Some are more meaty than others, but this is an advantage for most families. Use wingtips, giblets and any trimmings to make stock.

Grilled Lemon Chicken

8 chicken pieces
3-4 tablespoons butter
2 tablespoons lemon juice
1/2 teaspoon paprika

4 servings

Pat or wipe chicken pieces dry. Arrange them, skin side down, in a shallow baking dish (a sponge roll tin) lined with foil. Pieces should fill pan completely for minimum spattering. Preheat grill. Heat together butter, lemon juice and paprika. Using a small paintbrush, paint chicken pieces with warm mixture. Place tray under grill so that chicken is about 6 inches (15 cm) away from heat. Grill for 15 minutes, then turn chicken, skin side up, brush with more mixture and with liquid already around chicken and grill 15 minutes longer. Chicken is cooked as soon as juice runs clear (not pink) when flesh is pierced deeply with a sharp knife. Skin should be well browned at end of cooking time, but the pan must be far enough from the heat to cook the flesh without burning skin.

Brush with drippings during last 5 minutes of cooking, if necessary. Serve hot or cold.

When grilling with gas, place chicken on the bottom of the grill pan and lower the heat so that the cooking and browning times are similar to that above (about 30 minutes).
Grilled chicken is unbelievably juicy! Always line the pan with foil to save a messy wash up later.

Orange Chicken

1 chicken, jointed
¼ cup flour
3-4 tablespoons butter
1 clove garlic
1 teaspoon soy sauce
½ teaspoon salt
¼ teaspoon freshly ground nutmeg
1½ cups canned orange juice
1 tablespoon chopped parsley

4-6 servings

Joint chicken and coat pieces in flour (shake in plastic or paper bag). Brown pieces evenly in butter in a large frying pan over high heat. When browned, pour off any extra fat, and turn down heat. Add sliced garlic, soy sauce, salt, nutmeg, and orange juice. Cover pan and cook for 20 minutes, or until chicken is tender, turning pieces once or twice during this time. There should be just enough liquid left at the end of the cooking time to glaze the pieces of chicken. Leave the lid off the pan just before serving to concentrate the glaze if necessary, or add a-little water or stock if mixture dries out before meat is cooked. Chicken is cooked when juice runs clear (not pink) when flesh is pierced deeply with a sharp knife. Serve on rice or noodles.

VARIATION: Replace orange juice with pineapple juice. Add pineapple pieces towards end of cooking time if desired.

For special occasions garnish orange chicken with glazed mandarin segments. After chicken has been removed from pan, add ½-1 cup of drained mandarin segments, and 2 or 3 tablespoons liquid over high heat. Tilt pan until segments are coated with pan drippings. Spoon these over chicken, then dust with chopped parsley or decorate with parsley sprigs.

Bagged Golden Chicken

1 can (2 cup size)
  pineapple pieces
  or rings
1 packet cream of
  chicken soup
2 teaspoons soy
  sauce
6-8 chicken pieces

3-4 servings

Drain juice from pineapple and make up to 1 cup with water. Tip into roasting bag with soup powder and soy sauce. Squeeze bag to mix ingredients. Add chicken pieces and pineapple, tie bag loosely, stand it in a shallow dish and bake at 350°F (180°C) for 1 hour. Turn bag after 30 minutes so both sides of chicken are covered with sauce. Serve on rice or noodles, or with baked potatoes. Sprinkle with chopped parsley.

VARIATION: Pineapple pieces (or rings) may be added 10 minutes before serving, if preferred.

No mess, no fuss, no dirty dishes to wash after cooking — this recipe couldn't be simpler, because everything is mixed and cooked in one of the tough, clear bags for oven use. If you don't have a bag, and want to try the recipe, use a casserole dish with a very tightly fitting lid, increase the cooking time by 15 minutes, and be prepared to add more liquid during cooking, if mixture looks dry.

Crunchy Fried Chicken

6 chicken pieces
1/4 cup flour
1 egg
1-2 teaspoons water
1/2 teaspoon salt
1/2 teaspoon celery salt
1/2 teaspoon garlic or onion salt
1/2 cup fine dry breadcrumbs or rolled oats

3-4 servings

Pat or wipe chicken pieces dry. Measure flour into a paper or plastic bag and shake chicken in it. Beat egg, water and seasonings until blended. Tip out any remaining flour from the bag and replace it with the breadcrumbs.

Dip floured chicken into the egg, then shake in the breadcrumbs. Leave to stand for 5 minutes on a dry bench or wire rack. This is not essential but helps to set the coating.

Meanwhile, heat clean oil or cooking fat in a large frying pan. Have it 1/2-1 inch (2-3 cm) deep, and heated to 350°F (180°C) in an electric pan. Fry pieces, turning until evenly browned, for about 15 minutes, then cover the pan and cook about 10 minutes more, until the juice runs clear, not pink, when flesh is pierced deeply with a sharp knife.

Serve immediately, or keep warm for a short time in an oven heated to 250°F (120°C), or serve cold.

Grandmother's Chicken Stew

4-6 pieces chicken
¼ cup flour
2-3 tablespoons butter or oil
1-2 rashers bacon
4-6 small onions
1-2 carrots
1-2 stalks celery
1½ cups water
1 tablespoon instant chicken stock
3-4 small potatoes
cornflour and water paste
1-2 tablespoons chopped parsley

2-3 servings

Pat chicken pieces dry. Coat with flour and brown evenly in butter or oil in a large frying pan on high heat. Push chicken to one side and add chopped bacon and whole onions. Leave carrots whole if small and young, or cut in chunks or thick slices if older. Cut celery in 1-2 inch (3-5 cm) lengths. Add to chicken, cook 1-2 minutes longer, turning once, then lower heat, add water, chicken stock powder, and peeled potatoes. Cover and simmer for 30 minutes until chicken and vegetables are tender. Thicken stock with cornflour paste, season carefully with salt and pepper, and sprinkle with chopped parsley.

VARIATIONS: Add mixed herbs or thyme if desired, and add ¼ cup cream or evaporated milk before thickening.

Replace all or part of the water with white wine.

Chicken and Mushroom Casserole

6-8 chicken pieces
¼ cup flour
2-3 tablespoons butter or oil
1 clove garlic, sliced
1 cup (or can) button mushrooms
1 cup white wine or water
½ teaspoon salt
¼ teaspoon thyme
¼ cup cream
1 tablespoon chopped parsley

3-4 servings

Pat or wipe chicken pieces dry. Coat with flour (by tossing in a bag). Brown evenly in butter or oil in a hot frying pan. Pour off most of the remaining fat, then lightly brown the garlic and (drained) mushrooms. Add wine or water and salt, scrape pan to remove any pan drippings and pour over chicken pieces in a casserole. Sprinkle with thyme. Cover tightly and bake at 350°F (180°C) for 1 hour. Just before serving pour in cream, mix with gravy, season carefully, and spoon over chicken. Sprinkle with finely chopped parsley and serve immediately.

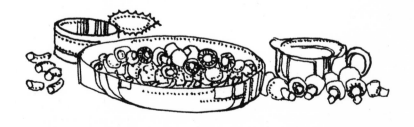

49

Quick Chicken Fried Rice

1-2 cups cooked chicken meat
1-2 rashers bacon
1-2 tablespoons butter or oil
1 clove garlic
2 onions, sliced
1 cup sliced mushrooms (optional)
1-2 red or green peppers, sliced (optional)
1 cup thinly sliced celery (optional)
2 tablespoons instant chicken stock
1 tablespoon soy sauce
2 tablespoons sugar
$1/2$ cup water
2-3 cups cooked long grain rice

3-4 servings

Slice chicken meat with a sharp knife. Chop bacon finely and cook it in a large frying pan until crisp. Remove from pan. Add butter or oil to bacon fat then add thinly sliced garlic, onions, mushrooms, peppers and celery. Cover and cook for 3-5 minutes, until vegetables are tender-crisp. Add chicken meat. Mix together instant stock, soy sauce, sugar and water. Add to vegetables and chicken. Stir to mix then add well drained cooked rice. Serve as soon as rice has heated through. Garnish with chopped spring onions or stir 1-2 finely shredded lettuce leaves through mixture just before serving. Sprinkle with crisp bacon.

Uncooked chicken breast meat may be used instead of cooked chicken. Remove skin from meat, chill it in a freezer or icebox, then cut it into very small pieces. Cook until it turns milky in the butter then add the remaining ingredients. Cook the rice carefully because the mixture will be a failure unless the grains are firm and separate.

Vegetables

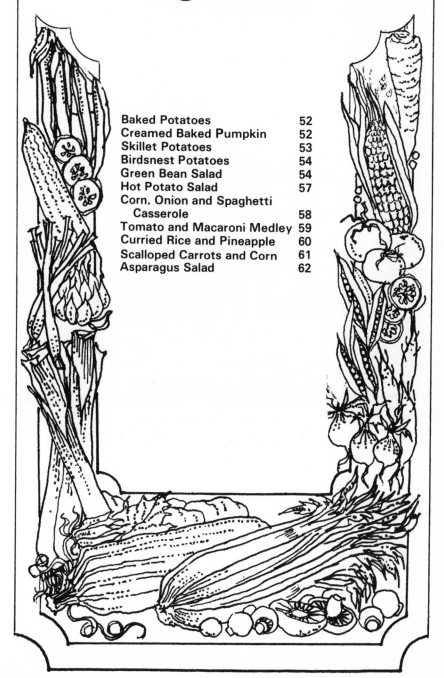

Baked Potatoes

Select medium sized potatoes with unblemished skins. Scrub clean, then coat with oil, melted butter or cooking fat to keep skins soft. Stand directly on a wire rack and bake at 400°F (200°C) for 40-60 minutes, depending on size. Do not prick — vegetables are cooked when they feel soft when pressed. Cut a cross in the top, then press gently until the points open. Top each with a cube of cheese or butter, or a spoonful of sour cream. Garnish with paprika, parsley or chives.

Creamed Baked Pumpkin

pumpkin
onion or garlic salt
cinnamon
brown or raw sugar
cream

Cut pumpkin into small cubes. Sprinkle with onion or garlic salt, cinnamon, and brown or raw sugar. Pour cream over pumpkin (use about ½ cup cream to 2 cups pumpkin). Cover tightly and bake at 350°F (180°C) for 45-60 minutes. Turn once or twice during cooking. Sprinkle with chopped parsley before serving.

Skillet Potatoes

4 potatoes
2 onions, sliced
3-4 tablespoons butter

4 servings

Peel and slice the potatoes into a bowl of cold water. Slice the onions and toss them in the butter in a large frying pan with a lid. Drain potatoes, and pat them dry, then add to the onions, and turn to coat with butter. Cover and cook over low heat for 10-15 minutes, turning occasionally, then raise heat so that vegetables brown slightly, and cook for 10-15 minutes longer.

Before serving, drain off any excess butter, season carefully with salt and pepper and sprinkle with finely chopped parsley. Serve with chops, hamburgers or cold meat.

This very simple potato dish is very popular with my husband and children. It is a mixture which cannot be hurried — the vegetables must be tender before they start to brown. To avoid frustrations when you make it, check that your frypan has a really smooth surface and is well seasoned so the vegetables will not stick. Clean pan with steel wool, then rub with salt on a paper towel or crumpled newspaper. Put a little oil in the pan and leave it to stand over a low heat for 5-10 minutes or longer, then remove excess, and cook the potatoes.

Birdsnest Potatoes

Scrub or thinly peel potatoes, then grate them on to an old tea towel. Squeeze cloth to remove all liquid. Sprinkle lightly with seasoned or plain salt then drop in handfuls on to a very hot pan containing enough oil or clean fat to cover the bottom.

Flatten cakes lightly but do not pack down. Turn when golden brown, and serve as soon as second side is cooked.

NOTE — Use old potatoes in preference to new ones. Grate just before use, since potatoes brown on standing.

Green Bean Salad

Cook double the quantity of tender, young, green beans required for one meal. Reserve the cooking liquid. Serve half the beans. To every cup of hot, remaining beans, add 2 tablespoons each of sugar, vinegar and bean liquid. Stir until sugar has dissolved, then add 1 tablespoon oil, ½ teaspoon salt, and freshly ground pepper.

Refrigerate until required, then drain and serve. (Use dressing once more, if desired.)

Hot Potato Salad

2-3 rashers bacon
1 onion, chopped
2 teaspoons flour
1 teaspoon sugar
$\frac{1}{2}$ teaspoon salt
$\frac{1}{2}$ teaspoon mustard
$\frac{1}{2}$ cup water
$\frac{1}{4}$ cup vinegar
4 cooked new, or waxy, potatoes
1-2 gherkins or dill
pickles, sliced, optional

3-4 servings

Cook the bacon slowly until it is crisp and golden brown then remove it from the pan. Cook the onion in the bacon fat until it is tender, but not brown, then add the flour, sugar, salt and mustard. Add water, mix well, and stir over low heat until smooth, then add the vinegar and boil again. Slice potatoes into sauce, and heat through, turning occasionally. Add finely chopped gherkins (or other pickles) to the potatoes, if desired, then sprinkle with chopped parsley and the crumbled crisp bacon and serve with sausages or cold meat.

This recipe can be kept warm for quite a long time, or can be reheated in the pan, if a small amount of water is added to thin it down. It is nicest when made with new potatoes. If old potatoes are used it is best to simmer or steam them in their jackets, and peel them after cooking.

Corn, Onion and Spaghetti Casserole

6-8 oz (175-225 g) spaghetti (uncooked)
2 tablespoons butter
2 medium onions
2 tablespoons butter
2 tablespoons flour
1 cup unsweetened condensed milk
½ cup liquid from sweet corn
salt, pepper and sugar
½-1 cup sweet corn
½-1 cup cheese, grated

6 servings

Cook the spaghetti until tender in plenty of boiling salted water. Drain and rinse with cold water.

Melt the butter in a large frypan, slice the onions in rings ¼″ (5 mm) thick and cook gently in the butter until tender but not brown.

Melt the second portion of butter in a medium saucepan. Add the flour then the milk and sweet corn liquid, ½ cup at a time. Boil and stir between additions. Season carefully with salt, pepper, sugar and seasoned salts, if desired, or add celery seeds, herbs, etc.

Arrange spaghetti, onions, sweet corn and cheese in a casserole dish in layers, covering them with sauce, or mix them carefully together in the sauce. Cover the casserole. Reheat in a moderate oven at 350°F (180°C) for 30 minutes or until heated through in the middle. Garnish with sliced tomatoes 10 minutes before serving (to let tomatoes heat through). Sprinkle with chopped parsley.

Tomato and Macaroni Medley

6 oz (175 g) macaroni*
6 cups water
2 teaspoons salt
3-4 large firm tomatoes
1 large onion, chopped
2-3 tablespoons butter
1 teaspoon instant beef stock
1 teaspoon sugar
1 teaspoon cornflour
$\frac{1}{2}$ cup water
$\frac{1}{4}$ cup chopped parsley

4-6 servings

Cook macaroni in boiling salted water for 8 minutes or until just tender. Dip each tomato into boiling liquid, then into cold water, to peel them easily. Meanwhile, chop onion into pieces the size of the macaroni and cook in the butter until tender but not browned. Mix together beef stock, sugar, cornflour and the second measure of water. Stir into onions, and simmer until sauce thickens. Chop skinned tomatoes and add to sauce with drained, cooked macaroni. Sprinkle thickly with chopped parsley (and a little basil if desired), stir over gentle heat for 1-2 minutes, then serve as a vegetable, with grilled chops or sausages.

*Macaroni is made in different shapes and sizes. Choose one of the wider tubes for this dish.

Curried Rice and Pineapple

¹/₂ teaspoon curry powder
¹/₂ teaspoon garlic or onion salt
1 tablespoon pineapple juice
2 cups cooked long grain rice
¹/₂-1 cup drained crushed pineapple
¹/₂ cup raisins or sultanas
1 small carrot, grated
3-4 spring onions, chopped

4-6 servings

Mix curry powder and seasoned salt with pineapple juice, then toss cooked rice in this. Mix in drained pineapple and sultanas, grated carrot, and half the spring onion. Refrigerate in a covered container, up to 2-3 days.

To serve:

(a) Mix oil and vinegar dressing, and extra pineapple juice if desired, with salad, and top with remaining chopped onions.

(b) Top with remaining onions and serve with mayonnaise thinned with pineapple juice.

(c) Dampen mixture with a little pineapple juice and heat through in a low or moderate oven. Serve hot, sprinkled with remaining onions.

This is a versatile mixture, as it may be served hot or cold. I make it when I have plain rice left over. It is only as good as the cooked rice, of course. I cook 1 cup of long grain rice (the parcooked variety) in 8 cups of boiling water with 1 tablespoon of salt. As soon as the grains are tender I drain the rice, rinse it, and transfer it to a roasting bag so that I can refrigerate it, then reheat it in the oven without dirtying any dishes.

I make my curried rice mixture in the same roasting bag too. I serve it cold with fish, meat and egg salads and hot with pork, chicken or sausages.

Scalloped Carrots and Corn

3-4 tablespoons butter
2 onions, chopped
3 tablespoons flour
$^1/_2$-1 teaspoon curry powder
1 teaspoon salt
1 teaspoon sugar
1 cup milk, or milk and liquid from corn
1 cup cooked or canned whole kernel corn
1 cup carrots, diced and cooked
1 tablespoon butter
1 cup stale bread, diced very small

6 servings

Melt the butter. Add the chopped onion, stir, cover, and cook gently for 5 minutes until tender but not browned. Add flour, curry powder, salt and sugar. Add the liquid in three portions, boiling and stirring well between additions. Fold in the corn and carrots to the cooked sauce. Turn into an ovenware dish.

Melt the remaining portion of butter. Remove from heat and toss bread cubes in it. Spread the buttered bread cubes over the vegetables.

Bake uncovered, in a moderately hot oven (375°F or 190°C) for 30-45 minutes. Serve with grilled meat or poultry and a green salad.

I have found that this simple casserole is always very popular when I serve it as a vegetable at a buffet party.
It can be prepared in advance then heated in a moderate oven with no attention during this time. It doesn't spoil if it has to wait for late arrivals either, so it is a useful dish.

Asparagus Salad

16-20 spears of asparagus
   (canned or freshly cooked)
1 tablespoon vinegar
1 tablespoon lemon juice
½ teaspoon salt
¼ teaspoon mustard
¼ cup corn oil
2 tablespoons fresh or cultured
   sour cream
1 tablespoon chopped parsley or chives
1 hardboiled egg, chopped
   or ½ red pepper, sliced.

4 servings

Drain asparagus (but do not let it dry out). In a medium sized bowl mix the vinegar, lemon juice, salt and mustard. Using a fork, whisk or rotary beater, beat the mixture while adding the oil slowly. Continue beating while adding the cream. Chop the chives or parsley very finely and stir in to the dressing.

Arrange asparagus on a platter or on individual small plates (keep heads pointing in same direction). Spoon dressing over asparagus, and garnish with chopped hardboiled egg, or strips of red pepper (or pimento).

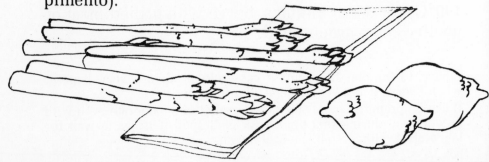

Lunch Dishes

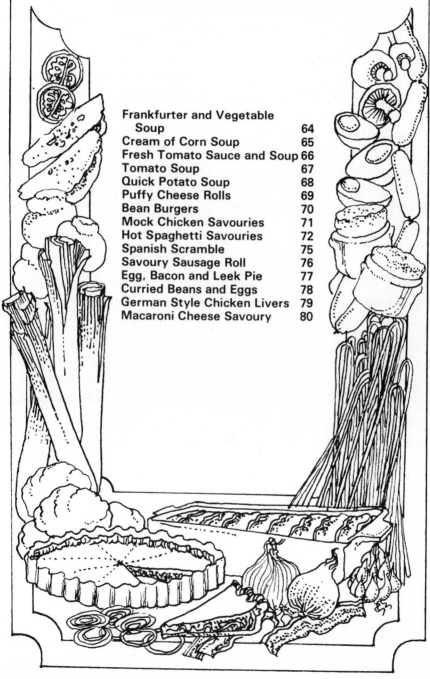

Frankfurter and Vegetable Soup

1 onion, sliced
1 stalk celery, sliced
1 carrot, grated
1 slice pumpkin or
marrow, grated
1 jerusalem artichoke,
grated
1 cup finely chopped
cabbage
2-3 tablespoons butter or
oil

4 cups water
2 teaspoons instant
chicken or beef stock
1 pkt cream of chicken, or
onion soup powder
2 cups cold water
3-4 frankfurters, sliced
pepper to taste
chopped parsley

6 servings

Chop or grate all vegetables very finely, and cook them in the butter or oil, stirring frequently, for 5 minutes. Do not let vegetables brown in this time. Add water, instant stock (or salt) and pepper, cover and simmer for 15 minutes, or until vegetables are tender. Mix packet soup with remaining water, add to vegetables and return to boil. Simmer 15 minutes longer and adjust seasoning. Five minutes before serving add the sliced frankfurters, and heat through.

Serve soup in bowls or mugs, sprinkled thickly with chopped parsley.

All sorts of vegetables may be used in this soup. I make it during the autumn, when there are many to choose from. Thinly sliced green beans, and chopped cauliflower make good additions. Diced, skinned tomato looks pretty. Add it with the packet soup. Do not grate potato into the soup, or it will thicken it too much. Add finely diced potato with the other vegetables, if desired.

Cream of Corn Soup

1 small onion, chopped
1 stalk celery, chopped
1 small carrot, chopped
1 slice fresh root ginger (optional)
1 tablespoon butter or oil
3 cups water
2-3 teaspoons instant chicken stock
1/2 teaspoon sugar
1-1 1/2 cups creamed corn
cornflour
1-2 spring onions, chopped

4 servings

Chop the onion, celery, carrot and ginger, and add to the hot butter or oil, in a medium sized saucepan. Cook for 2-3 minutes, but do not brown, then add water and instant stock, cover, and simmer for 20-30 minutes, until vegetables are very tender, then strain them out, and discard them.

Add sugar and creamed corn, simmer for 2-3 minutes, thicken with cornflour paste to the consistency you like it, taste and adjust seasoning carefully. Just before serving, add very finely chopped spring onion.

VARIATIONS: Add frozen prawns or sliced lobster to the soup with the spring onions, if desired.

Pour soup into individual dishes on top of 1-2 tablespoons of cooked rice.

Replace the water, vegetables and instant stock with chicken stock, if it is available. Dilute this if necessary, since chicken flavour should not be too strong in the final mixture.

Fresh Tomato Sauce and Soup

4 lb (2 kg) tomatoes, halved
or chopped roughly
3-4 tablespoons butter
1/2 cup water
1/2 cup red or white wine or
sherry and water
1 tablespoon instant beef or
chicken stock
2 teaspoons sugar
1 teaspoon salt
1 teaspoon black pepper
1 teaspoon nutmeg
1 bayleaf

pinch of tarragon
1/2 teaspoon dried thyme
1/2 teaspoon dried basil
or oregano
1/2 teaspoon dried
marjoram
1 spring parsley
1 onion, chopped
2 or 3 cloves garlic,
chopped
1 stalk celery, chopped
(optional)

Chop tomatoes roughly into a large saucepan with melted butter. Cook over medium heat, stirring frequently for 5 minutes, then add water and wine (if available). Add seasonings, using freshly ground pepper and nutmeg according to taste, then add whatever herbs you have. Chop the onion, garlic and celery roughly (I leave on the skins and leaves). Bring mixture to the boil, stirring occasionally, then cover and simmer 1/2-3/4 hour. Check every now and then to see the mixture does not catch on the bottom of the pan. Press pulpy mixture through a colander and discard the skins, herbs, etc. This quantity will make about five cups of well flavoured purée. Rinse out the saucepan in which the tomatoes boiled, and use it to make the thickened sauce.

Tomato Soup

2-3 oz (75 g) butter
½ cup flour
5 cups tomato purée

4 servings

Melt the butter, add the flour, and stir over low heat for 2-3 minutes. Do not hurry this step or your sauce and soup may have a raw flavour. Add 2 cups of the tomato mixture, and bring to the boil, stirring constantly. Add half the remaining tomato, boil again, then add the rest. Simmer for 5 minutes.

This sauce is excellent over chops, sausages, spaghetti and other pasta dishes, stuffed marrow, etc.

To convert it to soup, thin 2 cups of sauce with 1 cup of barely salted vegetable stock, any meat stock (especially poultry stock) or instant beef or chicken stock. I do not add milk to make a cream soup, but prefer to pour the soup, thinned with stock, on to 1-2 tablespoons of cream in individual plates.

Serve soup very hot, with lots of freshly fried or baked croutons, or a spoonful of whipped cream and chopped parsley.

For a good flavour, most of the tomatoes must be bright red, but it doesn't matter if they are a bit spotted, split, or marked by insects. After I pick the tomatoes, I pick a sprig of nearly every herb I pass to add to my 'brew', but this, of course, is a matter of taste.

Quick Potato Soup

2 onions sliced thinly
3-4 tablespoons butter
3 medium sized potatoes, diced
1 rasher of bacon, finely chopped
3 cups water
1 ½ tablespoons instant chicken stock
1 teaspoon sugar
pepper and nutmeg
mint and parsley
thyme or basil

4 servings

Slice the onions thinly and cook them in the butter in a saucepan over medium heat, for 3 minutes, until they are lightly browned. Peel and dice the potatoes, chop the bacon, and mix with the onion, then add the water, instant stock, sugar, and a little pepper and nutmeg. Add a sprig each of mint and parsley, and a pinch of thyme or basil, cover, and simmer until potatoes are tender.

Put mixture through a blender, foodmill or sieve. Adjust seasoning if necessary.

Serve soup sprinkled with paprika or chopped parsley, with small cubes of fried bread, or spoonfuls of whipped cream.

I am always a little wary of soups 'made from nothing'. I have a horror of soups that have no flavour. This one, however, is simple, quick, and very well flavoured. I like to put it in a blender, because this makes it so smooth. The flavour of the various herbs should not overpower that of the potatoes — and no one flavour should predominate.

Try this soup with toasted cheese sandwiches for a quick lunch on a cold day.

Puffy Cheese Rolls

6 bread rolls
butter, softened
8 oz (225 g) cheese, grated
$\frac{1}{2}$ teaspoon salt
$\frac{1}{2}$ teaspoon worcester sauce
$\frac{1}{2}$ teaspoon baking powder
2 eggs
2 tablespoons milk (approx.)

Split the rolls. Arrange, cut side down on the griller rack, and toast the crusty side until brown. Turn rolls and butter them.

Prepare the filling by combining the cheese, seasonings, baking powder and egg yolks in a medium sized bowl. Mix with a fork, adding enough milk to make the consistency that of creamed butter. Beat the egg whites to a stiff foam, then mix with the cheese and egg until thoroughly combined.

Spread the filling nearly to the edge of the rolls and grill about 4 inches from the heat till puffy and golden brown. Serve immediately.

This glamorised version of toasted cheese sandwiches makes a quick and tasty lunch dish.

Bean Burgers

2 eggs
$\frac{1}{2}$ cup grated cheese
1 onion, grated
2-3 rashers of bacon
$\frac{1}{2}$ teaspoon salt
$\frac{1}{2}$ (16oz or 450g) can baked
   beans in tomato sauce
4-5 hamburger buns

Beat the eggs with a fork until whites and yolks are barely mixed. Add the cheese, onion, bacon, salt and beans, and mix until coated with egg. Halve the buns and spread filling on them thickly, so that edges of buns are covered or they will burn. Stand them close together on a grill tray or sponge roll tin, and grill for 10 minutes, adjusting the heat so the buns do not burn before the filling sets.

VARIATION: Add mixed herbs, or basil and marjoram for extra flavour.

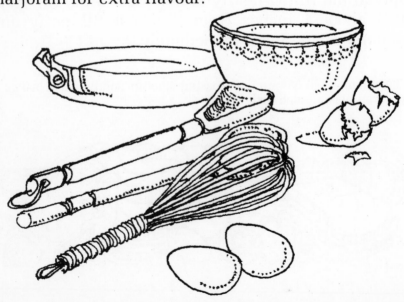

Mock Chicken Savouries

2 tablespoons butter
1 medium onion, finely chopped
2 teaspoons chopped parsley
$1/4$ - $1/2$ teaspoon dried mixed herbs
2 eggs
1 medium tomato

Melt the butter in a small saucepan, and add the finely chopped onion. Mix well, then cover the saucepan and cook gently for 3-4 minutes, until it is tender but not brown. Add the chopped parsley and dried herbs (use a little fresh thyme, sage and marjoram instead, if you have them growing). Remove from the heat and break in the two eggs. Add the diced tomato at the same time.

Mix the eggs through the other ingredients and return saucepan to the heat. Cook gently, stirring all the time, until the egg cooks and the mixture thickens. This should take from 1-3 minutes. Remove from the heat and cool before using.

For quick canapes, slice bread thinly, spread it thinly on both sides with soft butter or margarine, -remove the crusts and cut each slice into four small squares. Put these to brown on both sides in an electric frypan heated to 350°F (180°C). Adjust heat of pan if necessary so bread cooks slowly, and is an even golden brown on both sides. Spoon a little filling in to each canape, and top with a slice of gherkin, radish or olive.

(Rectangular crisp bread slices, sprinkled with garlic salt before baking, make good bases for drained sardines, too. Garnish them with parsley and grated lemon rind.)

71

Hot Spaghetti Savouries

6 slices thinly cut bread
butter
3 eggs
½ cup tasty cheese
1 onion, very finely sliced
2-3 slices bacon, chopped
½ (16 oz or 450 g) can spaghetti
   in tomato sauce

Cut crusts from bread, and butter carefully, spreading it right to the edges. Cut each slice into four quarters and press each piece, butter side down, into a muffin pan.

Beat the eggs with a fork, just enough to combine whites and yolks, then add remaining ingredients. Stir well to mix, and divide the mixture between the 24 bread cases.

Bake at 375°F (190°F) for 15-20 minutes, until the cases are golden brown, and the filling set. Serve immediately.

These savouries seem popular with everybody. Serve them with soup for an easy lunch or produce them as a snack at any time of day for children of all ages.

Quick Potato Soup (p. 68)

Spanish Scramble

1 large onion, chopped
1 green pepper, diced
2 tablespoons oil or butter
1 (16 oz or 450 g) can spaghetti
   in tomato sauce
3 eggs
2 tablespoons milk
1/2 teaspoon salt
shake of pepper

4 servings

In a large frying pan, over medium heat, cook the chopped onion and green pepper in the oil or butter until they are tender, but have not browned. Add spaghetti. Beat the eggs, milk, salt and pepper together, and pour it over the hot spaghetti.

Lift the spaghetti with a fish slice so the egg mixture can run underneath and cook, but do not stir the mixture more than necessary. Serve as soon as the egg has set.

Garnish with chopped spring onions, green pepper rings or quartered tomatoes, if desired.

Savoury Sausage Roll

Pastry
2 cups flour
1 teaspoon salt
4 oz (125 g) butter
½ cup water approx.

10 servings

Filling
1 lb (450 g) sausagemeat
3 eggs
1 packet onion or
  mushroom soup
1 onion, finely chopped
½ cup fine, dry
  breadcrumbs
1 can (16 oz or 450 g)
  baked beans in tomato
  sauce

Sift the flour and salt together. Cut or rub in the butter until the mixture resembles breadcrumbs. Add the water, a little at a time, tossing mixture with a fork, until the dough particles will stick together to make a firm dough. Leave to stand in a cold place for 5 minutes, then roll out 12-15 inches (30-38 cm) square.

Put all the filling ingredients together in a bowl, reserving a little egg. Stir to mix. Lay the pastry on a sponge roll, or other shallow tin, or on a piece of foil on an oven slide, and put the filling in a sausage shape down the middle of it. Dampen top and sides of pastry with water. Fold the top and bottom of the pastry over the sausagemeat, then the sides so they overlap at the top. Decorate with any pastry scraps and brush with reserved egg.

Bake at 375°F (190°C) for 45-60 minutes and serve hot or cold, with tomato sauce.

When you have to serve large numbers on a low budget, try this sausage roll.

Egg, Bacon and Leek Pie

Pastry
1 ½ cups flour
1 teaspoon salt
3-4 tablespoons butter
2-3 tablespoons lard
  (or extra butter)
6 tablespoons very
  cold water

Filling
4-6 slices bacon
5-6 eggs
1 cup cooked, sliced
  leeks
salt, pepper

6 servings

To make pastry cut the fat into the sifted flour and salt until the mixture resembles coarse breadcrumbs. Add the water slowly while tossing the mixture with a fork. Use just enough water to make the dough particles stick together to form a stiff dough. Cover and chill for at least 15 minutes.

Roll out thinly to form two circles 10-12 inches (25-30 cm) in diameter. Handle the dough carefully to avoid stretching it. Line a 9 inch (23 cm) pie plate with one circle. Trim the edges.

Fry or bake the bacon until cooked. Cut into pieces about an inch (2-3 cm) square. Put ⅓ bacon into the uncooked shell. Break in three eggs, and add another ⅓ of the bacon, the drained leeks, and salt and pepper. Add the remaining eggs and bacon. Break one egg and reserve part of it for glazing top of pie. Brush the edge of the lower crust with cold water. Put the upper crust in place. Fold the edge of the top crust under the edge of the bottom crust. Decorate or flute the edges. Cut 2-3 holes in the pastry, and glaze with beaten egg.

Bake in the middle of a hot oven 425°F (230°C) for 15 minutes or until the pastry starts browning, then in a moderate oven, 350°F (180°C) for 20-30 minutes until the filling is firm. Serve hot or cold.

Curried Beans and Eggs

4-6 eggs, hardboiled
2 onions, sliced
1-2 apples, sliced
2-3 tablespoons butter or oil
1 teaspoon curry powder
1 (16 oz or 450 g) can baked
  beans in tomato sauce
1/2 cup water
2 teaspoons instant beef stock
1-2 teaspoons cornflour
chopped parsley

6 servings

Put eggs to hardboil.

Chop onions and apples into small pieces, and brown in butter or oil. Add curry powder, cover, and leave over very low heat for 5 minutes, or until onion is tender. Add baked beans, water and instant stock, mix gently but thoroughly, and simmer over very low heat for 15 minutes to blend the flavours. Thicken mixture with a little cornflour paste, if necessary.

Shell and halve or quarter the eggs. Heat through if necessary and garnish with chopped parsley.

VARIATION: Serve the curried beans without the eggs, as accompaniments to grilled or pan fried sausages or chops.

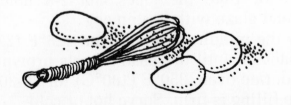

German Style Chicken Livers

2 oz (50 g) butter
1 onion, chopped
2 apples, peeled and diced
1 lb (450 g) chicken livers
2 tablespoons flour
½ teaspoon salt
shake of pepper
½ teaspoon dried thyme

4 servings

Melt butter in a large frying pan. Add the chopped onion and apple, and cook on medium heat until tender and lightly browned. Remove from pan, wipe pan clean and return it to stove to heat.

Halve chicken livers, removing any fibres and blemishes, shake them in a plastic or paper bag with the flour, salt and pepper. Over high heat brown chicken livers, a few at a time, in the remaining butter, adding more if necessary. When all have been browned, put the apple and onion back in the pan. Add thyme, and cook over gentle heat for 3-5 minutes. Add three or four tablespoons of water towards the end of this time, and turn mixture so it is lightly coated with glaze. Serve on rice or noodles.

VARIATIONS: Add the juice of half a lemon with the water. Sprinkle with chopped parsley.

Brown 1 or 2 rashers of chopped bacon with the onion and apple.

Macaroni Cheese Savoury

5 oz (150 g) macaroni
1/2-1 cup sliced celery (optional)
3 tablespoons butter
2 rashers bacon, chopped
2 onions, sliced
3 tablespoons flour
1/2 teaspoon salt
pepper and nutmeg
2 cups milk
1 cup grated cheese.

6 servings

Add macaroni and sliced celery to 8 cups boiling salted water. Boil gently, uncovered, until macaroni is tender (about 8 minutes).

Meantime, in a large frying pan, over medium heat, melt the butter and cook bacon and onion in it until onion is tender but not browned, about 5 minutes. Add flour and seasoning, then add milk, half a cup at a time, boiling between additions. Stir in cheese, then add cooked, drained macaroni and celery. Mix gently over very low heat for 2-3 minutes, and serve. If serving is delayed, thin sauce with extra milk.

Top each serving with extra grated cheese and paprika, if desired. Accompany with a tossed green salad or tomato salad, or fried tomatoes.

NOTE — Macaroni comes in different shapes and sizes. Use one of the larger sizes for this recipe.

Desserts and Puddings

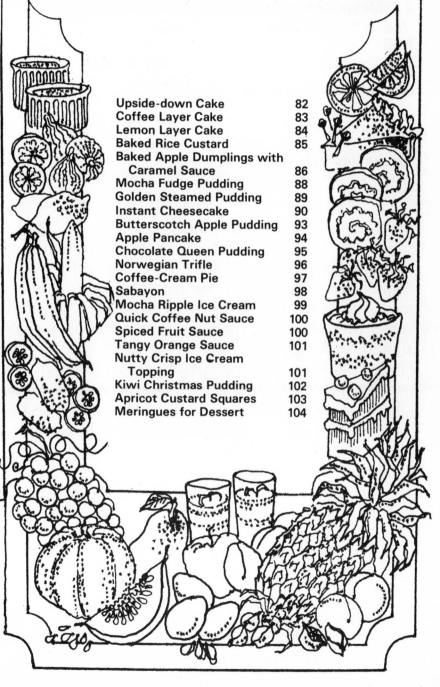

Upside-down Cake

Topping
2 tablespoons butter
¼ cup brown sugar
fruit*

Batter
3-4 tablespoons butter
⅓ cup sugar
1 teaspoon vanilla

½ teaspoon cinnamon
 (optional)
1 egg
1½ cups flour
2 teaspoons baking
 powder
¼ teaspoon salt
¼-½ cup milk

6 servings

*Suggested fruit
Cooked pineapple, peaches, pears, prunes, dried apricots, raw ripe apple, pears, bananas, plums.

Melt the butter for the topping in a tin 8″ (20 cm) square, 9″ (23 cm) round. Sprinkle the brown sugar evenly over the butter. Place well drained pieces of canned or cooked fruit, or fresh ripe fruit on this mixture. Place the fruit so it will look attractive when turned upside down — generally cut surfaces should touch the sugar.

Warm the butter until nearly liquid in a metal bowl or saucepan. Add the sugar, vanilla, cinnamon and egg, stand the bowl (or pan) in cold water, and beat until all ingredients are well mixed. Add sifted dry ingredients and milk alternately. The batter should be thin enough to be poured over the fruit. Since it spreads as it cooks, do not worry if it looks uneven before baking. Bake uncovered at 350°-375°F (180°-190°C) for 35-45 minutes, until golden brown and firm in the centre. Working quickly, while very hot, loosen the edges and turn cake upside down on a serving plate.

If you are not going to serve it immediately, invert tin over it, so that the topping does not dry out, and leave it to stand in a warm place for 15-30 minutes.

Coffee Layer Cake

**1 unfilled sponge sandwich 8 or
9 inches (20-23 cm) across
1 tablespoon instant coffee
³/₄ cup sugar
¹/₄ cup water
¹/₂ teaspoon rum or brandy essence
or 2 tablespoons rum or brandy
1 ¹/₂ cups cream, whipped
¹/₄ cup chopped walnuts or
chopped toasted almonds**

8 servings

Split each layer of sponge.

Boil instant coffee, sugar and water together, stirring constantly until sugar has dissolved completely, then simmer for 2 minutes, cool and add essence or spirits. Whip the cream.

Place a layer of sponge on a serving dish, drizzle one sixth of the syrup over it, then spread with a sixth of the whipped cream. Drizzle the same quantity of syrup over the next layer of cake while it is lying on the working surface, then place it, coffee side down, over the cream.

Repeat with remaining layers, then frost the sides and top of the cake with the remaining cream. Sprinkle nuts over side and top of cake. Refrigerate at least 12, but preferably 24 hours before serving. Cut in wedges.

This makes an excellent dessert for entertaining, since it can be prepared the night before you need it. It keeps well for 2 or 3 days, although the nuts may discolour the cream a little. If you like, pipe extra cream over the nuts an hour or so before serving, and decorate it with fruit.

Do not serve this cake only a few hours after you have made it. It needs at least 12 hours for the cake to absorb moisture from the cream and syrup.

Lemon Layer Cake

1 rectangular unfilled sponge sandwich
1 ¹/₂ cups milk
¹/₂ cup cream or top milk
1 packet lemon instant pudding
3-4 tablespoons marmalade

Line the sides and bottom of a loaf tin with foil. Split sponge to make four thin layers. Select a piece with an attractive surface for top of cake and cut it to fit loaf tin. Join pieces of sponge cake where necessary, but do not leave gaps with no cake at the ends of the tin. Measure milk and cream. Add instant pudding and beat for required time. (For best results, use milk at room temperature. Cold milk will produce a fluffier, light dessert.)

Select the sponge for the middle layer and spread it with half the marmalade. Pour half the setting pudding over the first layer of sponge, then cover it with the next piece of sponge, marmalade side down. Repeat with the remaining pudding and the third slab of sponge spread with the last of the marmalade. Fold ends of foil over cake and leave in a cool place for at least 15 minutes.

To serve, lift foil off cake and invert tin on serving plate, carefully lift off tin, then foil. Run knife along sides and ends of tin to smooth it.

Decorate top of cake with suitable fruit such as canned mandarin segments. Pipe rosettes of cream on either side of the fruit. Serve immediately, or refrigerate until needed.

VARIATIONS: Use instant puddings of different flavours, and change the jam accordingly.

little boiling water may need to be added towards the end of the cooking time. (If too much water evaporates from the sauce it becomes toffee-like as it cools.) Serve the apples hot, with the sauce spooned over them.

Remember that apples with the core removed cook much more quickly than those with the core cavity stuffed with dried fruit. It can be useful to remember this if you are running a little late.

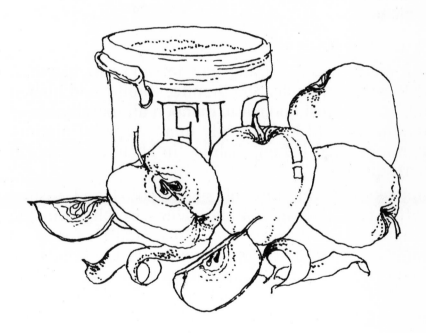

Mocha Fudge Pudding

1 cup flour
1 tablespoon cocoa
2 teaspoons baking
 powder
1/2 teaspoon salt
1/2 cup sugar
2-4 tablespoons chopped
 walnuts
1/2 cup milk
1 teaspoon vanilla
2 tablespoons butter,
 melted

Topping
3/4 cup sugar
1 tablespoon cocoa
2 teaspoons instant
 coffee*
1 1/2 cups boiling water

4-5 servings

*Replace all or some of
 this with equal
 quantities of cocoa, if
 desired.

Sift flour, cocoa, baking powder and salt together. Add sugar and nuts. Stir in milk, vanilla, and melted butter. Mix just enough to dampen all ingredients — mixture should look slightly lumpy. Spread mixture into a greased baking dish or tin about 9 inches (23 cm) square.

Sprinkle the mixture of sugar, cocoa and instant coffee over it. Pour boiling water carefully over the topping. Bake uncovered at 350°F (180°C) for 45-60 minutes, or until firm in the centre. While it bakes, a thick chocolate sauce forms under the crust. Spoon some of the sauce over each serving, and accompany with a generous scoop of vanilla ice cream.

Golden Steamed Pudding

Batter
3-4 tablespoons butter
¼ cup sugar
½ teaspoon vanilla
1 egg
1¼ cups flour
2 teaspoons baking powder
2-3 tablespoons milk

Topping
1-2 tablespoons brown sugar
¼ teaspoon cinnamon
½ cup (approx) drained stewed fruit

6 servings

Prepare a basin for steaming. Butter the bottom and sides, spread the brown sugar and cinnamon on the bottom, and arrange the well drained fruit on it. Melt the butter in a metal bowl or saucepan. Add the sugar, vanilla and egg and beat with a rotary beater until light coloured. Stand the bowl in cold water if necessary. Add the sifted flour and baking powder, with enough milk to form a batter soft enough to drop from the spoon. Pour the batter on top of the fruit. It should half fill the basin, so that there is plenty of room for rising. Cover the basin with two layers of greaseproof paper and secure it with string (loop a piece of string across the top so the pudding can be lifted out easily) or cover it with aluminium foil, leaving enough to pinch securely under the rim of the bowl or lie smoothly against its side.

Lower the pudding into a large saucepan ⅓-½ full of boiling water. As a precaution against burning if the water evaporates, stand the pudding basin on a piece of crumpled foil, an old saucer, or a rack. Cover. Boil gently, adding extra boiling water when necessary, for 1½-2 hours. Lift out pudding, run a knife around side and unmould it.

Instant Cheesecake

1 cup cream cheese
1 cup milk
1 lemon instant pudding
¼ cup fruit juice (approx)

8 servings

Empty carton of cream cheese into a medium sized bowl and beat it with a wooden spoon until it becomes creamy, and easy to work with. Beat in about a quarter of the milk, gradually, then pour on the rest of the milk, sprinkle instant pudding powder over this, and beat briefly with a rotary beater until combined. If mixture becomes too thick, add a little fruit juice to thin it down.

Use cheesecake filling to fill a crumb crust (see page 97) or a baked shortcake shell.

OR split the two halves of an unfilled sponge cake, use half the mixture between the halves, and the remaining mixture on top.

Decorate any of the above with well drained cooked fruit, or ripe fresh fruit.

Glaze fruit with light coloured jam, thinned with a little fruit syrup, then brought to the boil, if desired.

Decorate with piped whipped cream, if desired. Serve immediately.

(Filling may be kept for 1-2 days, but is at its best eaten half an hour after it is made).

This recipe is faster than any cheesecake mix that I know, because it is firm enough to serve after it is beaten for less than 30 seconds.

I like the flavour of the cheesecake made using lemon instant pudding — but you can use vanilla, chocolate, butterscotch and mocha flavours too.

Butterscotch Apple Pudding

1 cup flour
2 teaspoons baking
 powder
1/4-1/2 teaspoon nutmeg or
 ginger
1/2 teaspoon salt
2-3 cooking apples, diced
1/2 cup milk

Topping
1 cup brown sugar
1/2 teaspoon cinnamon
2 tablespoons butter
2 cups water

5-6 servings

Sift flour, baking powder, spice and salt together. Peel and core apples, cut them into 3/4 inch (2 cm) cubes, and toss in the flour mixture. Add the milk and mix with a knife to blend all ingredients. Spread mixture into a greased baking dish or tin, about 9 inches (23 cm) square.

Measure the topping ingredients, in the order given, in a saucepan, and bring to the boil. Pour boiling mixture carefully over batter in pan.

Bake uncovered, at 375-400°F (190-200°C) for 45-60 minutes, until topping is firm in the centre, and golden brown. As pudding bakes, a butterscotch sauce forms under the apple-studded crust. Serve pudding warm, with some of the sauce spooned over each serving, with vanilla ice cream or cream.

Self saucing puddings are easy to prepare, and provide a well flavoured inexpensive and filling dessert for hungry children in cooler weather.

Make the most of your oven. To save fuel, brush potatoes (or sweet potatoes or kumara) with cooking fat or oil and bake them alongside the pudding. Did you know that most vegetables (other than leafy green ones) can be baked in a tightly covered casserole dish (or a roasting bag) with a little water, a shake of salt and pepper, and a tablespoon of butter? They take about twice as long to bake (around 375°F or 190°C) as they do to boil.

Apple Pancake

2 tablespoons sugar
1 teaspoon cinnamon
2 tablespoons butter
2 medium apples, sliced
2 egg yolks
2 tablespoons milk
3 tablespoons flour

$1/2$ teaspoon baking powder
$1/4$ teaspoon salt
2 egg whites
3 tablespoons sugar

3-4 servings

Mix the sugar and cinnamon together. Melt the butter in a 9-10″ (23-25 cm) metal handled, heavy bottomed frying pan. Sprinkle the cinnamon sugar evenly over the melted butter. Peel and quarter the apples. Cut each quarter into 3 or 4 slices, then arrange all the slices neatly on the cinnamon sugar, working towards the centre. Leave to cook over low heat for 5 minutes while mixing the batter.

Separate the eggs into two bowls. Add the milk to the yolks, stir to mix, then stir in the flour, baking powder and salt which have been sifted together. Beat the egg whites until foamy, add the sugar and beat to a stiff foam (i.e. until the peaks turn over). Fold the whites into the yolk mixture, carefully but thoroughly. Spread the batter evenly over the hot apples in the pan.

Bake in a hot oven 400°F (200°C) for 10 minutes, till puffy and golden brown. Loosen the edges and invert pancake on to a flat serving plate. Serve immediately with cream or ice cream.

This is a quick and unusual dessert. You can start to make it only 20 minutes before you plan to serve it. Cook it in a frying pan which has a metal handle, or in a shallow flame resistant dish, because the initial cooking is on top of the stove, but it is finished off in a hot oven.

Tangy Orange Sauce

2 tablespoons brown sugar
2 tablespoons custard powder
1 tablespoon butter

1 cup canned or
fresh orange juice

Mix brown sugar and custard powder in a medium sized saucepan. (Use cornflour if custard powder is not available.) Add juice and butter. Bring to the boil, stirring constantly. Serve warm, over ice cream.

VARIATIONS: Dilute juice with water for blander sauce. Fruit salad sauce: Replace some of the orange juice with pineapple juice. Stir in sliced banana and passionfruit pulp as soon as sauce has finished cooking.

Nutty Crisp Ice Cream Topping

2 tablespoons butter
2 tablespoons brown sugar
2 tablespoons white sugar

$1/2$-$3/4$ cup rolled oats
2 tablespoons chopped
  nuts

Melt butter in an electric frypan at 350°F (180°C). Add all remaining ingredients and heat for 4 or 5 minutes, flattening mixture with a fish slice and stirring constantly to prevent lumps forming. Topping is cooked when sugar has melted and caramelised, and has coated the oats.

Spread hot mixture on clean paper or a shallow tin to cool. Store in an airtight tin. Sprinkle over ice cream (and cooked fruit).

Kiwi Christmas Pudding

¹/₂ cup mixed fruit, chopped
³/₄ cup water
2 tablespoons vinegar
¹/₂ teaspoon cinnamon
¹/₂ teaspoon mixed spice
¹/₄ teaspoon ground cloves
¹/₂ cup sugar
2 tablespoons butter
1 tablespoon cornflour or
vanilla custard powder
1-2 tablespoons brandy or
¹/₂ teaspoon brandy essence
1 round, unfilled sponge cake
1 quart (litre) vanilla ice cream
red and green cherries

Use a commercial fruit mixture, or make a mixture of your own, including some cherries and peel. Wash fruit if necessary, then chop (use a wet knife to stop fruit sticking to it). Put first six ingredients into a medium sized saucepan, bring to the boil, then simmer over low heat for 3-5 minutes. Add sugar and butter, then the cornflour or custard powder mixed to a paste with ¼ cup cold water. Bring mixture to boil, stirring constantly, then remove from heat. Leave mixture to cool a little, then stir in brandy, or brandy essence. Taste mixture and add more if desired. Use sauce immediately, or cover and rewarm just before use.

Place sponge on a flat serving plate. Sprinkle with brandy and/or sherry and/or fruit juice. Using a scoop or spoon heated in very hot water make ice cream balls and pile them on sponge. Pour warm sauce over ice cream and decorate with red and green cherries.

Apricot Custard Squares

3 cups flour
½ teaspoon salt
6 oz (175 g) butter
1 (30 oz or 850 g) can
   apricot halves or pieces
½ cup sugar

1 teaspoon cinnamon
3 eggs
1 cup syrup drained from
   apricots
1¼ cups unsweetened
   condensed milk

Sift flour and salt into a large bowl, then rub in butter until crumbly.

Press this dry mixture into a 9 inch (23 cm) square tin. (Use a tin with a loose bottom, or line the bottom and 2 sides with aluminium foil, so cooked square can be lifted out easily.) Drain apricots well, and arrange the fruit over the crumbly base, so it is evenly covered. Cut fruit into pieces if necessary. Mix sugar and cinnamon, and sprinkle evenly over fruit. Bake at 350°F (180°C) for 20 minutes.

Beat eggs, syrup from apricots and unsweetened condensed milk until blended, but not foamy. (Replace unsweetened condensed milk with fresh cream, or cultured sour cream if desired.) Pour over hot apricots, and bake for 30 minutes longer, or until custard has set in the middle. Serve hot, warm or cold, with whipped cream.

NOTE — Use 1-1½ cups of the milk or cream and alter the quantity of syrup so total liquid remains the same.

From the hostess's point of view this recipe is good because it is reliable — it always works, and it can be made whenever time allows. It can be prepared and cooked just before it is to be eaten, or it can be made up to a day ahead, and served cold, or reheated. It is not a suitable dessert for freezing, because of its custard top.

Meringues for Dessert

4 egg whites
¼ teaspoon salt
1 cup castor sugar

Beat the whites and salt to a stiff foam (i.e. until the peaks turn over). Add the sugar gradually and beat until the mixture forms peaks which are quite stiff, and the mixture is smooth.

Pipe the meringues on to aluminium foil or dampened greaseproof paper, using a star-shaped nozzle, or spoon them, using two dessert or teaspoons. Cook in a very cool oven, 250°F (120°C) for 1-1½ hours until they are dry.

(a) Crush the meringues and mix them with whipped cream 5 minutes before serving them on cooked fruit or sweetened raw berries.

(b) Cover the bottom of a round dish with drained cooked fruit. Put a layer of custard over the fruit. Arrange meringues around the edge of the dish, with or without whipped cream. This looks like a pie.

(c) Flavour part of a meringue mixture. For coffee meringues dissolve 1 teaspoon coffee in a small amount of boiling water for each egg white used. Fold the coffee into the beaten meringue mixture. Top each coffee meringue with slivered almonds before baking. Fill with cream and serve with coffee.

(d) Make large flattened nest-shaped meringues using the back of a spoon to form the hollows, or using a piping bag to make piped edges. Fill these with sweetened fruit, flavoured cream, ice cream or custard filling.

In Betweens

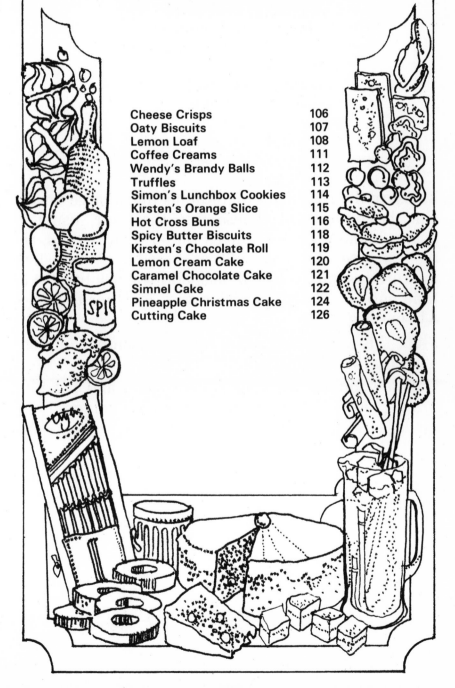

Cheese Crisps

1 ½ cups flour
5 oz (150 g) cold butter
1 ½ cups grated cheese
1 ½ teaspoons baking powder
½ teaspoon salt
½ teaspoon mustard
½ teaspoon paprika
shake of pepper
cold water

Measure the first eight ingredients into a large bowl. Cut the butter and cheese into the flour, using a pastry blender or two knives rather than fingers, so the mixture stays as cold as possible. When the mixture resembles rolled oats, add water a little at a time until the dough particles stick together to make a firm dough.

Flour this lightly and roll it out thinly and evenly on a lightly floured board.

Cut into squares, rectangles or fingers, and bake at 375°F (190°C) for 10-15 minutes or until golden.

Lift onto a rack with a spatula or fish slice and leave to cool.

Serve buttered or plain, with a cup of tea or with drinks.

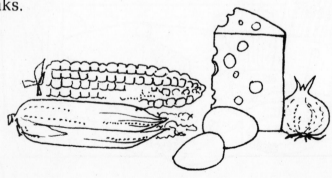

Oaty Biscuits

4 oz (100 g) butter
1/2 cup (100 g) brown sugar
1/2 cup (50 g) flour
1 1/2 cups (125 g) rolled oats
1/2 teaspoon salt

Soften but do not melt the butter, add the sugar and beat until free from lumps. Add the remaining ingredients and mix well. Chill the dough to firm it, for easier handling, if the weather is warm.

Place the dough on a lightly greased oven tray, cover it with greaseproof paper or plastic film and roll it out 1/4 inch (5 mm) thick.

Remove the film. Mark the dough into rectangles or squares, but do not move the pieces on the tray. As the mixture does not rise much, the pieces can touch each other.

Bake at 350°F (180°C) for 10 minutes, or until the biscuits are lightly browned. Cut pieces free if necessary. Lift them carefully off the tray with a spatula while hot, and cool them on a wire rack. Store in an airtight tin.

Serve plain or buttered.

Although these biscuits keep well in an airtight tin, they are best the day they are made.

These biscuits are plain but are sweet enough to appeal to children. Butter them to have with tea or coffee, or sandwich them together for packed lunches.

Lemon Loaf

3 oz (100 g) butter
³/₄ cup sugar
1 lemon, grated rind and juice
2 eggs
1 ¹/₂ cups flour
1 teaspoon baking powder
¹/₂ teaspoon salt
¹/₂ cup milk
¹/₂ cup chopped walnuts
   or raisins
   or sultanas
¹/₄ cup sugar

Cream the butter and sugar. Grate in the lemon rind then add the eggs one at a time, beating well between additions. Sift together the flour, baking powder and salt, and add them, alternately with the milk, to the creamed mixture. Stir in nuts or raisins. Turn into a loaf tin about 9 x 5 inches (23 x 13 cm) which has had the bottom and two long sides lined with a sheet of greaseproof paper.

Bake at 350°F (180°C) for an hour, or until the sides of the loaf shrink from the sides of the tin and a skewer in the middle of the loaf comes out clean.

Mix the lemon juice with the sugar (do not heat) and sprinkle, spoon or pour this over the top of the hot loaf. Return the loaf to the oven for 1 minute, then remove, lift on to the rack (by lifting the paper) and leave to cool.

Slice when cold, preferably the day after baking. Serve buttered or plain.

The crunchy, sweet-sour topping on this loaf makes it interesting and different.

Caramel Chocolate Cake (p.121)

Kirsten's Orange Slice

3 oz (100 g) butter
³/₄ cup (¹/₂ a can)
    sweetened
    condensed milk
1 cup coconut
grated rind from 1 orange
    or tangelo

1 packet (7 oz or 200 g)
    wine biscuits, crushed

Orange icing
1 cup icing sugar
2 tablespoons soft butter
orange or tangelo juice to
    mix

Melt the butter in a medium sized saucepan. Add the condensed milk and stir until well mixed, then remove from heat. Stir in coconut, orange rind, and biscuit crumbs. (Crush biscuits in a paper bag or plastic bag with a rolling pin. Crumbs should be even and fairly small. Crumbs made in a blender tend to be too fine for this slice.)

Press mixture lightly into a greased shallow tin such as a sponge roll tin, so it is about ¼ inch (15mm) thick. It does not matter if the mixture does not fill the whole tin.

Measure icing sugar and butter into a medium sized bowl. (Do not have butter liquid, but have it warm enough to mix.) Add a few drops of juice at a time, until icing is spreading consistency. Spread it thinly over the slice then run a fork in wavy lines over it, so that the biscuit mixture shows through. Leave to set in the refrigerator then cut in rectangles and store in a tin with greaseproof paper between the layers.

Kirsten likes this slice in her school lunch, so she makes it quite often. She got quite a shock when I suggested that she work out what it cost to make, then compared the price with Simon's lunch box cookies!

Hot Cross Buns

2 tablespoons dried yeast   5-6 cups flour (approx.)
1/2 cup water   1 teaspoon cinnamon
1 tablespoon sugar   1 teaspoon mixed spice
2 tablespoons butter   1/4 teaspoon ground cloves
1/2 cup sugar   1 cup sultanas or currants
1 egg   2 tablespoons mixed peel
1 cup milk

As soon as you decide to make the buns, mix the dried yeast, lukewarm water and sugar and leave it in a warm place to start working while you assemble the other ingredients, utensils, etc.

In a large stainless steel bowl, melt the butter, add the sugar, egg and milk. Beat to blend, then add the yeast mixture. Stir in 3 cups of the flour, the spices, and the dried fruit. Beat vigorously with a wooden spoon for 1-2 minutes then cover the bowl with a damp cloth, or a piece of foil, or put it in a large plastic bag and leave it in a warm place until it rises to double its bulk. (Suitable warm places include a warm sunny concrete or wooden doorstep or porch, a sink of warm water, or an electric oven preheated at lowest heat then turned off.) The time needed for this will depend on the temperature and the freshness of the yeast. It should take 45-60 minutes, but may take longer. For best results, do not proceed until dough has risen enough.

Stir risen dough with wooden spoon, and add enough of the remaining flour to make a dough firm enough to knead.

Turn out on to a floured board and knead until the dough looks smooth and satiny and springs back when poked with a finger. At the beginning of the kneading the board must be kept well floured or the dough will stick but as it is kneaded, although it looks moist, it does not stick. Do not add more flour than necessary — dough should be as soft as possible.

Cut kneaded dough into thirds. Use each third to make a tin of buns. (I find I get better buns if I put them fairly close together in cake tins, rather than on sideless trays. They join as they cook but can be easily broken apart.)

Grease the cake tins. Use 8 inch (20 cm) square, 9 inch (23 cm) round, or ring tins.

Cut each piece of dough in 9 or 16 parts. Form these into balls and arrange them in the tins.

Cover tins with foil, or put the tins in plastic bags. Leave in a warm place until they have risen to twice their size. Then put a short pastry cross on each bun. (Make pastry, roll out very thinly, brush all over the top with water, and cut into strips. Arrange strips, wet side down, diagonally, on risen buns.)

Bake at 400°F (200°C) for 12-15 minutes. As soon as centre buns feel firm, and crust against the tin is golden, lift from the oven and brush with a syrup made by boiling 3 tablespoons sugar with 2 tablespoons water.

Replace buns in oven for 30 seconds if you think the syrup needs to dry out, then cool in tins until cool enough to handle, and turn out. Serve buns hot, warm or reheated.

NOTE — These buns freeze well. Take them out of their tins and put them in a roasting bag as soon as they are cold. Suck all air from the bag, and freeze immediately. Thaw and reheat buns in a moderate oven, without taking them from their bag.

Replace dried yeast with the same quantity of compressed (or baker's)yeast if it is available. This is slightly less than one small foil packet.

Spicy Butter Biscuits

8 oz (225 g) butter
1 cup (packed) brown sugar
1 egg, separated
2 cups flour
3 tablespoons cinnamon
1 teaspoon ginger
4-5 dozen almonds

6-8 dozen biscuits

Cream the butter and sugar. Separate the egg, and add the yolk and a quarter of the white to the dough. Sift the flour, cinnamon and ginger together (remember to use level standard cup and spoon measures — mixture is spoilt if too much flour is used). Stir into creamed mixture, then chill to make dough easy to handle.

Roll out a quarter of dough at a time, 1/8-1/4 inch (3-5 mm) thick, then cut into rounds with a fluted cutter.

Place biscuits carefully on a very lightly oiled or buttered oven tray. Blanch and halve the almonds and turn them in the bowl of egg white. The egg white should not be bubbly, but should be beaten with a fork just enough to make it of even consistency. Place one or two almond halves, flat side down, on each biscuit, and brush a little egg white on the middle of each biscuit to glaze it.

Bake at 350°F (180°C) for 10 minutes, or until biscuits darken slightly. Lift carefully on to rack. Biscuits should become very crisp on cooling.

Store in an airtight tin.

The quantity of cinnamon in these biscuits *is* three tablespoons — it's not a misprint! Nor has the baking powder been left out — the biscuits do not rise.

Kirsten's Chocolate Roll

3 eggs
¹/₂ cup sugar
¹/₂ cup flour
2 tablespoons cocoa
1 teaspoon baking powder
1 tablespoon boiling water

Beat eggs and sugar together until mixture is very thick and creamy. For best volume, have eggs at room temperature, rather than straight from the refrigerator.

Sift flour, cocoa and baking powder on to the egg mixture, then fold them in carefully but thoroughly. Add boiling water and mix again. Spread mixture evenly on a sponge roll tin lined with greaseproof paper.

Bake at 425°F (230°C) for 8-10 minutes, or until the centre of the sponge springs back when pressed lightly with a finger.

Working quickly, loosen the sponge from the sides of the tin, and turn it out on to a clean piece of fine cotton (muslin or an old tea towel) that has been wet, then rung out as dry as possible. Lift off paper from bottom of sponge, and roll sponge and tea towel together, lightly but firmly. Roll either way, depending whether a short thick roll, or a long thin one is wanted. Stand roll, still in towel, on a rack until cold then unroll carefully, spread with raspberry jam and whipped fresh cream or mock cream, and roll up again — without the cloth!

Sprinkle with icing sugar just before serving.

Kirsten asks for this cake for every birthday party she has. It is quick but delicious — remember, level, standard measures.

Lemon Cream Cake

2 eggs
1 cup sugar
1 cup cream
grated rind of 1 lemon
2 cups flour
2 teaspoons baking powder

Measure eggs, sugar and cream into a medium sized bowl and beat until thick and creamy. Grate the lemon rind finely, over the mixture, then fold in the sifted flour and baking powder.

Have ready an 8 inch (20 cm) square tin or a 9 inch (23 cm) round tin. Grease the sides and line the botton with butter paper, turn mixture into prepared tin and bake at 350°F (180°C) for 45 minutes or until the centre springs back when pressed with a finger.

When cold, ice cake with lemon butter icing made using the juice from the grated lemon. If desired, split cake in two and fill the centre with a mock cream filling. If cake is to be eaten immediately it can be filled with whipped cream.

VARIATION: Replace lemon rind and juice with finely grated tangelo rind and juice.

This cake is a cross between a sponge cake and a buttercake. Cream replaces butter and milk and although it may seem extravagant, it costs only a few cents more. Because the cream is already liquid, there is no need to bother with softening or creaming, so it is quick and easy.

Watch that you do not use heaped measures of flour, and don't overcook the cake, or it will tend to dry. It is best eaten within two or three days.

Caramel Chocolate Cake

4 oz (125 g) butter
³/₄ cup sugar
2 tablespoons golden syrup
2 eggs
1 teaspoon vanilla
2 cups flour
¹/₂ teaspoon baking soda
2 teaspoons baking powder
¹/₂ cup milk
2 tablespoons cocoa
1 tablespoon milk

In a medium sized saucepan melt the butter. When liquid, add the sugar and golden syrup and stand over very low heat until the syrup has mixed with the sugar and butter. Stir, but do not boil. Cool saucepan in cold water and add eggs and vanilla. Beat with a fork to mix. Sift flour, baking soda and baking powder into mixture in saucepan. Pour in milk, then mix thoroughly with a fork to blend the flour and milk with the rest. The batter should be thinner than a normal butter cake mixture — just thin enough to pour.

Pour half the mixture into an 8 inch (20 cm) square or 9 inch (23 cm) round tin lined with buttered paper.

To the remaining mixture add the cocoa and milk, and stir to mix. Pour this layer carefully and evenly over the caramel one. Bake at 350°F (180°C) for 45 minutes until a skewer in the middle comes out clean.

When cold, ice with chocolate icing.

Simnel Cake

Almond Paste

4 oz (100-125 g) ground
  almonds
½ cup castor sugar
1 cup icing sugar
½ teaspoon almond
  essence
beaten egg to mix

Simnel Cake

8 oz (225 g) butter
1 cup (packed) brown
  sugar
1 teaspoon mixed spice
4 eggs
2 cups flour
1 teaspoon baking
  powder
1 lb (450 g) mixed fruit
8 oz (225 g) sultanas or
  currants
almond paste
water icing

Mix the almonds and sugars in a bowl. Add the essence and enough beaten egg to make a dough that is stiff enough to handle. Knead this lightly then roll it out on floured greaseproof paper to make two circles to fit the tin used. (Save the remaining egg to glaze the top layer of paste as it bakes.)

Cream the butter and sugar in a large bowl, until the mixture is light coloured and fluffy. Add the mixed spice and one egg and continue beating. Sift the flour and baking powder and clean and sort the dried fruit if necessary. Sprinkle half the flour mixture over the fruit and mix thoroughly to coat the fruit. Add 1-2 tablespoons of the remaining flour to the creamed mixture, then break in another egg. Spoon in more flour before the other eggs are added, to make sure the mixture does not curdle. After all the eggs have been added, tip in the rest of the flour and fruit and stir thoroughly to mix.

Spoon a little more than half the cake mixture into an 8 inch or 9 inch (20-23 cm) diameter round cake tin that has been lined with greaseproof paper. Level off the mixture and put one circle of almond paste over it. Spoon the remaining mixture over this. Bake at 300°F (150°C) for three hours or until the centre of the cake feels firm and a skewer comes out clean (do not stick the skewer through the almond paste layer).

Remove the cake from the oven and raise the heat to 350°F (180°C). Stand the hot cake on a board or rack and cut the greaseproof paper to the level of the cake. Brush the top of the hot cake with apricot or other light coloured jam, then put the remaining circle of almond paste on this. Pat it down so that it is thinner in the middle and thick at the edge, then pinch the edge to make a raised border like the edge of a pie shell.

Brush the edge with the egg left over from making the paste. Return the cake to the oven and bake for 10-15 minutes, or until the fluted edge is lightly browned. Cool the cake.

When cool decorate by mixing a half cup of icing sugar with a few drops of water, lemon juice and green food colouring. Spread this thinly over the surface of the cake. Decorate with (a) an Easter chicken and candy eggs, or (b) almond paste balls arranged in a circle near the edge of cake.

A simnel cake is a fruit cake in which a middle layer of almond paste is baked. Traditionally it was eaten during Lent, but it is now regarded as an Easter cake. The cake mixture itself is not as rich, dark or fruity as a Christmas cake, but has more the consistency of a 'family sultana cake'. As soon as the cake comes out of the oven another layer of almond paste is put on top and its edge is crimped rather like the edge of a pie-crust.

Only home-made almond paste made from ground almonds can be used in the cake, since commercially made almond icing (which usually contains almond flavouring and no ground almonds) can cause the cake to sink and become sticky.

Pineapple Christmas Cake

8 oz (225 g) butter
1 cup sugar
½ teaspoon vanilla
  essence
½ teaspoon almond
  essence
½ teaspoon lemon
  essence
1 teaspoon cinnamon
1 teaspoon ground ginger
1 teaspoon mixed spice
¼ teaspoon nutmeg
6 eggs

1 lb 8 oz (675 g) sultanas
1 lb (450 g) raisins
8 oz (225 g) currants
2 oz (50 g) preserved
  ginger
2 oz (50 g) cherries
2 oz (50 g) peel
2 oz (50 g) almonds
1 cup drained crushed
  pineapple
3 cups flour
¼ cup brandy

If you are using bulk-packed dried fruit, wash and clean the sultanas, raisins and currants, then spread them on a large roasting pan and dry them in the sun or a warm oven. This is best done the day before you plan to mix the cake. If desired, replace the sultanas, raisins, currants, cherries, ginger and peel with 3½ lb (1 kg 550 g) mixed fruit. This should not need washing.

Before mixing, line a 9 inch (23 cm) cake tin with 2-3 layers of paper, finishing with greaseproof paper. Have the paper higher than the sides of the tin to prevent rapid browning during cooking.

Cream butter and sugar until light and smooth, then add the essences and spices. Add the eggs one at a time, beating thoroughly after each addition to prevent curdling. (Add some of the measured flour if the mixture shows signs of curdling.)

Add the cherries, chopped ginger, peel, almonds, and well drained pineapple to the cleaned, dried fruit. Mix the fruit with the measured flour so that it is well coated.

Stir the fruit and flour into the creamed ingredients using a large (wooden) spoon. Use a little extra flour if necessary to produce a moist batter that will drop from the hand.

Turn into the prepared tin. Sprinkle with extra blanched almonds if desired. Bake at 300°F (150°C) for 2 hours, then at 250°F (130°) for 1½-2 hours longer, until a skewer inserted in the middle of the cake comes out clean.

Remove the cake from the oven and pour the brandy over it immediately. Leave to cool in the tin. When cool enough to handle, transfer to rack to finish cooling.

NOTE — Alter the proportions and types of dried fruit if desired, but keep the total weight the same.

Start thinking about your Christmas cake several weeks before Christmas. The flavour of the cake improves as the cake ages, and there are always 101 other things to think about as Christmas gets closer.

Rich cakes keep well in a cool storage place, but you may like to freeze your cake, months ahead. (Rich cakes seem even *better* after freezing.)

The high price of dried fruit means that a rich cake is quite an investment, so follow the recipe carefully. This is a fairly light cake with an excellent flavour. It contains no baking powder or baking soda, but you can add a teaspoon of baking powder with the flour, if it makes you feel happier.

Recently a lady rang in on a talk back radio programme to tell me she liked my pineapple cake and had made it successfully more than 200 times since I gave her the recipe — a recommendation for any cake!

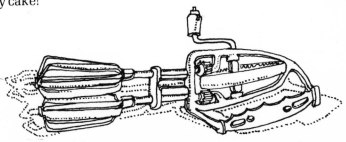

Cutting Cake

1 ½ tablespoons cornflour
1 cup cold water
1 lb (450 g) sultanas
8 oz (225 g) butter
1 cup sugar
½ teaspoon lemon essence
½ teaspoon orange essence
½ teaspoon vanilla essence
½ teaspoon almond essence
3 eggs
3 cups flour
2 teaspoons baking powder
½ teaspoon salt

Boil cornflour (or 2 tablespoons custard powder) and water until thick, then cool. Wash sultanas if necessary and drain well. Cream butter, sugar and essences, then add eggs, one at a time, beating well between additions. Sift the flour, baking powder and salt, and coat the drained sultanas with part of this. Add the remaining flour alternately with the cold cornflour mixture, to the creamed ingredients. Stir in the floured fruit. Turn into an 8 inch (20 cm) square or 9 inch (23 cm) round tin lined with greaseproof paper. Bake at 325°F (170°C) for 1½-2 hours, until a skewer in the middle comes out clean.

NOTE — If mixture shows signs of curdling while the eggs are being added, add a tablespoon of the measured flour after each egg.

This is a well flavoured family fruit cake. The essences add extra flavour, because no peel, cherries, etc are used — just sultanas. Replace the sultanas with mixed fruit and leave out some of the essences if you like.

Remember to use standard cup and spoon measures.

Pickled Pineapple (p. 135), Pineapple Chicken (p. 44) and Curried Rice and Pineapple (p. 61)

Preserves

Strawberry Jam

2 lb (1 kg) strawberries
¼ cup water
3 lb (1 ½ kg) sugar
2 teaspoons tartaric acid

Clean the berries and boil them with the water in a jam pan, crushing them with a potato masher as they cook. When the fruit is soft, add the sugar and bring to the boil, stirring frequently.

Boil briskly for 3 minutes then add the acid and stir well. Boil 4-5 minutes longer, then pour into cleaned, warm bottles. Seal when cold with paraffin wax and cellophane covers.

Note — While the jam is cooling in the jars, stir it carefully and gently with a skewer or fork to distribute the fruit evenly.

Use half recipe if desired, but do not use more than 2 lb (1 kg) fruit for each batch of jam.

For best results, add the acid after three minutes. Watch the colour change as you add it — it is quite surprising!

I don't make a lot of jam, but I *am* fussy about the little I do make.

I expect to produce a jam with a real, fresh fruit flavour, I want a bright, clear colour, and a texture which is not too runny but not too thick, with pieces of tender fruit evenly through a soft jelly.

For a good jam or jelly one must have the right proportions of sugar, acid and pectin — if one of these is lacking, failure will result.

Different fruits contain differing amounts of acid and pectin and water, so although a general recipe for jam may be followed, if you are fussy too, you will probably use slightly different proportions and modified techniques with each fruit for best results.

Raspberry Jam

3 lb (1 ½ kg) raspberries
3 lbs (1 ½ kg) sugar

Sort through raspberries and bring them to the boil in a jam pan. Add sugar immediately and bring mixture back to the boil over high heat, stirring frequently. Protect your hands with rubber gloves, and break up the fruit as it heats by beating with a rotary beater.

Let jam boil briskly for 3 minutes then turn off heat. Beat mixture with rotary beater several times during the next 5 minutes.

Pour into heated cleaned bottles. When cold seal with melted paraffin wax and cellophane covers.

Note — Increase cooking time to 5 minutes for firmer jam. Do not increase quantities, but make in smaller batches if desired.

Hints — Freeze bags of strawberries and raspberries without sugar for winter jam making. Follow these recipes using the thawed fruits.

Keep paraffin wax in an old teapot, heat it carefully (and gently) then pour over jam. When using jam, wash paraffin tops and replace in teapot for later melting down.

Never make jam in a small saucepan since long gentle heating (necessary to prevent boiling over) affects the quality of the final result.

Pear Mincemeat

4 lb (2 kg) ripe pears
2 cups seedless raisins
1/2 lemon
1/2 cup vinegar
3 cups sugar
2 teaspoons ground allspice
2 teaspoons cinnamon
1 teaspoon ground cloves
1 teaspoon ground nutmeg
1/2 teaspoon ginger

Clean pears and raisins. Remove seeds from lemon. Bring remaining ingredients to boil in a large saucepan. Mince cored but unpeeled pears, raisins and whole lemon; or grate pears, chop raisins and thinly slice then dice lemon, and add to spiced vinegar. Simmer for 30 minutes, stirring frequently. Pour into hot jars leaving 1/2 inch (2 cm) headspace, screw on boiled seals, and process in waterbath for 20 minutes. Remove screw tops from sealed jars after 24 hours. Store jars in a cool, well ventilated place. Use mincemeat in pies or tarts.

If you have ever lived in a house with a large and prolific pear tree in the garden, you will appreciate the difficulties of processing the crop.

We had three pear trees in our last garden. Since we never sprayed them, and always waited for the fruit to drop, our pears were far from perfect. I always felt that my bottled plain pears were not a first class product, so I tried out other pear preserves, where the quality of the fruit would not matter too much.

Pear mincemeat can be used in small pies or large tarts and pies. It's not as rich as the Christmas variety of mincemeat, and is more liquid, but it can be drained or thickened just before use. (Never thicken it before bottling.) It can also be thickened with custard powder or cornflour and served warm over plain, steamed, or other winter puddings.

Pear Ginger

1 cup crushed pineapple
2 lemons, grated rind and juice
6 cups sugar
4 lb (2 kg) diced raw pears
6 oz (175 g) preserved ginger

Measure the crushed pineapple, lemon rind and juice and sugar into a preserving pan. Remove the skins and cores from the pears and stand them in a bowl of lightly salted water to stop them browning. Weigh them about 1 lb (500 g) at a time, after preparation, then dice them into ½ inch (1 cm) cubes, and add them to the pineapple, lemon and sugar, stirring to coat the pieces.

Add the ginger, thinly sliced, and leave to stand for several hours, until the sugar has formed syrup. Boil, uncovered, for 2 hours, or until the syrup is thick — about the consistency of jam.

Pour into clean, heated jam jars and seal with paraffin wax and/or cellophane tops. It makes about 6 1lb (500 g) jars.

NOTE—Heat syrup to 220°F (105°C) if you have a candy thermometer.

This jam is rather like a good fruit salad jam. It is not too gingery for children, and is very popular with adults. Every time I make it, I worry that the mixture is too thin, and think it will never thicken. However, it always does, in the end.

You can use crystallised ginger, or ginger that has been bottled in syrup. If you live near a store that stocks the ingredients for Chinese cooking, buy a jar of red ginger. It tastes the same but looks twice as pretty!

For best results with this preserve, I used my later greenish honey pears — I think they were called 'Conference'. They were longer than my other pears and had a long thin part near the stem.

Passionfruit Honey

2 tablespoons butter
1 cup sugar
1 lemon, squeezed
1 teaspoon grated lemon rind
1/2 cup passionfruit pulp
2 eggs

Select a medium sized bowl you can stand over a saucepan of boiling water.

Stand it over the hot water, and measure into it the first 5 ingredients. When the sugar has dissolved, add the eggs which have been beaten just enough to mix the whites and yolks then poured through a sieve.

Stir constantly until the mixture thickens (5-10 minutes). Spoon into small sterilised jars, cover lightly until lukewarm then seal with melted paraffin wax.

Use passionfruit honey to fill small shortcrust tarts, to sandwich sponge halves, to spread on pavlovas, or serve with ice cream, or instead of jam, for table use.

I have received many letters asking for ideas for preserving passionfruit and lemons.

It is easy to freeze both by pouring the juice or pulp into ice-block containers, leaving them to solidify, then popping out the frozen cubes into a plastic bag, for freezer storage. Don't add sugar to the juice and pulp because a very sugary mixture will never freeze hard, and will be difficult to handle and store.

Other methods aren't so straightforward. It is hard to bottle small quantities of passionfruit unless you use an outfit equipped with tiny bottles and seals, or use small bottles and cover them with very heavy plastic film made for this purpose.

When I have lots of lemons I make lemon cordial, which keeps for months if carefully made and sealed.

Pickled Pineapple

1 can pineapple slices or pieces
¼ cup vinegar
½ cup sugar
4-6 whole cloves
¼ teaspoon cinnamon
¼ teaspoon ginger
pinch salt

Drain syrup from pineapple into saucepan containing remaining ingredients.

Simmer, uncovered, for 15 minutes (until liquid is reduced to 1 cup). Add pineapple, return to boil, then remove from heat.

Arrange fruit attractively in a straight sided jar. Fill with syrup. Refrigerate 24 hours before use.

Store in refrigerator.

NOTE — If you want to make a longer lasting pineapple pickle reduce the number of cloves, bottle in preserving jars, fill with spiced vinegar to within ½ inch (1 cm) of the top, seal with a boiled preserving seal as usual, and process for 10 minutes in a waterbath.

These are not true pickles, in that they will not keep indefinitely. They are, however, delicious and unusual, and may be stored for several weeks in the refrigerator. I always make them the day before I plan to serve them, although I feel they are probably at their best a day or two after this.

In the photograph opposite page 126 you will see how attractively the rings can be arranged in a jar. A straight sided jar, without a smaller lip, is easiest to fill. Jars like this, with glass or cork tops, make good gifts. Filled with homemade sweets or a pickle.they are better still!

Serve pickled pineapple with hot or cold meat — poultry, ham, roast pork — or even with sausages.

Herb Vinegar

fresh tarragon
and/or fresh dill
and/or fresh marjoram or
   oregano
and/or fresh thyme
and/or fresh chives
and/or fresh basil
1-2 cloves
1-2 peppercorns
1 clove garlic
1-2 teaspoons sugar
white or cider vinegar

Pick sprigs of fresh herbs (with leaves and/or seeds). Use several herbs together, or one type only. Push herbs into a clean bottle. Use 4-6 sprigs about 8 inches (20 cm) long for a bottle that holds 4-6 cups of liquid. Add cloves, peppercorns, garlic and sugar if desired, then fill bottle with white vinegar. Seal bottle with a cork or screw top, and stand in a warm sunny place for 2-3 weeks, shaking bottle about once a day.

Then pour liquid into another bottle. Place one or two fresh herb sprigs in bottle for ornament, then seal with corks or screw-on plastic tops.

If flavour is too strong, dilute before use with plain vinegar.

I enjoy making flavoured vinegars. I make herb vinegar at the end of the summer, when my herbs have run riot, and spiced vinegar at any time of the year. I find that these vinegars add interesting flavours to sauces, dressings and pickles.

Spiced Vinegar

4 cups cider or white vinegar
1/2 cup sugar
1 tablespoon whole black peppers
1 teaspoon whole cloves
2 teaspoons whole allspice
1/2-1 teaspoon whole nutmeg, grated
1 1/2 teaspoons celery seed
1 teaspoon mustard seed
1/2 teaspoon ground ginger
1 clove garlic, sliced

Heat vinegar and sugar almost to boiling point. Measure remaining ingredients into a quart preserving jar. Pour hot vinegar over spices and cover with screw-on plastic lid. After 24 hours remove the garlic. Leave in a warm place for 2-3 weeks, shaking occasionally, then pour off vinegar from spices and bottle. Seal bottles with corks or screw-on plastic tops.

Tomato Ketchup

12 lb (6 kg) tomatoes, chopped
3 large onions, sliced
1 clove garlic, sliced
3 tablespoons pickling spice
1 teaspoon celery seed
1/2 teaspoon dried basil (optional)
1/2 teaspoon dried marjoram (optional)
1/3 cup salt
6-8 cups sugar
2 tablespoons glacial acetic acid

Chop ripe red tomatoes roughly, without skinning them, into a very large saucepan or jam pan.

Slice onions and garlic thinly and add to tomatoes. Place pickling spice, celery seed, basil and marjoram in a muslin bag, leaving plenty of room for spices to expand during cooking. Tie bag securely, and add to tomatoes. If tomatoes are firm, add about 1/2 cup of water to prevent them sticking as they start to cook. Boil, uncovered, for 1 hour, then add plain (non-iodised) salt and sugar, and stir until mixture returns to the boil. Press liquid through a colander or coarse sieve, and discard the solids.

Bring sauce back to boil, add acid, and boil for 5 minutes. Pour hot sauce into bottles which have been carefully washed, rinsed, then heated in a very low oven for about 30 minutes. Seal bottles with plastic screw tops which have been washed then had boiling water poured over them, or with boiled corks. Dip corks in wax when bottles cool.

Glacial acetic acid may be bought from the chemist. Treat it carefully — don't sniff it because it is very strong — and keep it on a high shelf out of reach of small children.

8 cups sugar makes rather sweet sauce very popular with children.

Pineapple Chutney

2 large onions, chopped finely
2 cups crushed pineapple
2 cups sugar
2 cups white or cider vinegar
2 teaspoons curry powder
2 teaspoons turmeric
2 teaspoons salt
2 tablespoons flour

Chop onions into small pieces. Place in large saucepan with crushed pineapple, and simmer until onion is tender. Add sugar and nearly all the vinegar and bring to the boil. Mix remaining ingredients to a thin paste with the last of the vinegar, add to boiling mixture, stirring until it thickens. Taste, and add more curry powder if desired. Simmer for 10-15 minutes, until thick, then pour into clean, hot jars and seal with paraffin wax.

This pickle can be made quickly and easily, at any time of the year. With cheese, it makes good sandwiches and topping for crackers. It also makes an excellent dip for a meat fondue.

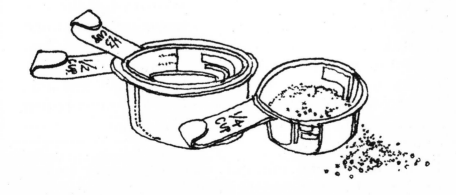

Bread and Butter Pickles

10-12 cups thinly sliced cucumbers
6 onions, sliced
½ cup salt
4 cups sugar
1 tablespoon mustard seed
2 teaspoons celery seed
1-2 teaspoons turmeric
4 cups white vinegar
  or
4 cups water and 3 tablespoons
  glacial acetic acid.

Slice the cucumbers into a large plastic or stainless steel bowl or measuring jug. Add the thinly sliced onions and salt, then cover with cold water, stir to mix, and leave for 12-24 hours. Drain well.

In a large saucepan or jam pan mix the sugar, mustard seed, celery seed and turmeric. (Use the larger quantity of turmeric if a bright yellow colour is desired.) Add the vinegar and bring liquid to the boil, stirring to dissolve the sugar. Add drained cucumbers and heat until liquid boils again. (Do not boil mixture for longer time.) Have jars ready (sterilised in very hot water or in the oven). Prepare lids ahead by pouring very hot water over them and leaving them to stand in this until ready to use. Pour cucumber mixture into bottles leaving ¼"-½" (1 cm) at the top. Screw on lid firmly as each bottle is filled. Stand bottles on wooden board, newspaper or folded towels until cold, then wipe clean, and store in a cool dark place.

If you are strong minded, wait 1-2 weeks before using pickles. Keep opened jars in the refrigerator.

As its name implies, Bread and Butter Pickle is delicious on fresh bread and butter, alone or with meat filling. It is also good on crackers, alone or with cheese, and is an excellent accompaniment to cold beef, pork, lamb or poultry.

It keeps best (and crisp) in sealed jars. Since I like it in jars smaller than regular preserving jars, I use coffee jars and others with good plastic screw tops. Whenever I buy food in jars with lacquered metal lids with an inner'rubber' seal attached, I save them carefully as they can be reused and make excellent containers for pickles like this, or any other product that needs an airtight seal.

Whole Pickled Cucumbers

Select small freshly picked cucumbers or gherkins about 3-4 inches (7-10 cm) long. Clean them and soak them overnight in cold water. Drain and pack them loosely into clean preserving jars. (Top up jars with chunks or thick slices of cucumber if necessary).

Add to each quart (litre) jar:

1-2 sprigs dill
½ teaspoon mustard seed
6 peppercorns

In a large saucepan heat the following ingredients until the sugar and salt dissolve:

1 cup plain salt
1 cup sugar
20 cups water
4 tablespoons glacial acetic acid

Pour this over the cucumbers, leaving ½'' (1 cm) headspace. Cover with boiled seals, screw on bands tightly and boil for 5 minutes in a waterbath, with water at least 1 inch (2-3 cm) over the tops of the bottles. (Water will take some time to come to the boil). Store in a cool dark place for 6-8 weeks before using.

The quantity of liquid given overleaf will fill about 10 bottles, depending on the size of the cucumbers. Glacial acetic acid is obtainable from chemists. Keep it away from children as it is very strong.

These pickles are mild enough to eat whole. After the jars are opened they must be refrigerated, or they may ferment. There is never any danger of this in our house — unless I watch very carefully, the jar is emptied in one sitting!

For milder pickles, dilute brine with equal quantity of cooled boiled water after opening jar.

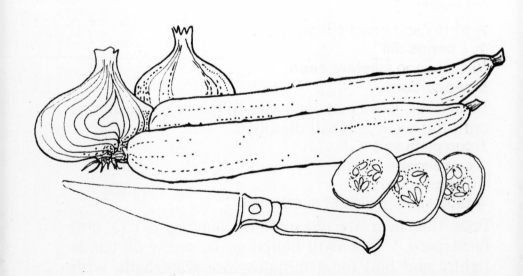

Index

143

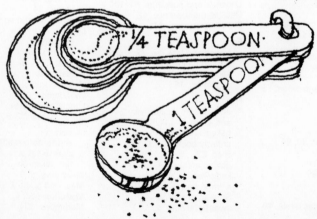

144